The Lord's Prayer

Our Father, who art in heaven,
  hallowed be thy Name,
  thy kingdom come,
  thy will be done,
    on earth as it is in heaven.
Give us this day our daily bread.
And forgive us our trespasses,
  as we forgive those
    who trespass against us.
And lead us not into temptation,
But deliver us from evil.
For thine is the kingdom.
  and the power and the glory,
  for ever and ever. Amen.

Our Father in heaven,
  hallowed be your Name,
  your kingdom come,
  your will be done
    on earth as in heaven.
Give us today our daily bread.
Forgive us our sins
  as we forgive those
    who sin against us.
Save us from the time of trial,
  and deliver us from evil.
For the kingdom, the power,
  and the glory are yours,
  now and for ever. Amen.

The Apostles' Creed

I believe in God, the Father almighty,
  creator of heaven and earth.
I believe in Jesus Christ, his only So
  He was conceived by the power
    and born of the Virgin Mary.
  He suffered under Pontius Pilate
    was crucified, died, and was b
  He descended to the dead.
  On the third day he rose again.
  He ascended into heaven,
    and is seated at the right hand
  He will come again to judge the
I believe in the Holy Spirit,
  the holy catholic Church,
  the communion of saints,
  the forgiveness of sins,
  the resurrection of the body,
  and the life everlasting. Amen.

El Padre Nuestro

Padre nuestro que estás en el cielo,
   santificado sea tu Nombre,
   venga tu reino,
   hágase tu voluntad,
     en la tierra como en el cielo.
Danos hoy nuestro pan de cada día.
Perdona nuestras ofensas,
   como también nosotros perdonamos
     a los que nos ofenden.
No nos dejes caer en tentación
   y líbranos del mal.
Porque tuyo es el reino,
   tuyo es el poder,
   y tuya es la gloria,
   ahora y por siempre. Amén.

Credo de los Apóstoles

Creo en Dios Padre todopoderoso,
   creador del cielo y de la tierra.
Creo en Jesucristo, su único Hijo, nuestro Señor.
   Fue concebido por obra y gracia del Espíritu Santo
     y nació de la Virgen María.
   Padeció bajo el poder de Poncio Pilato.
     Fue crucificado, muerto y sepultado.
   Descendió a los infiernos.
   Al tercer día resucitó de entre los muertos.
   Subió a los cielos,
     y está sentado a la diestra de Dios Padre.
   Desde allí ha de venir a juzgar a vivos y muertos.
Creo en el Espíritu Santo,
   la santa Iglesia católica,
   la comunión de los santos,
   el perdón de los pecados,
   la resurrección de los muertos,
   y la vida eterna. Amén.

A PRAYER BOOK
for
THE ARMED SERVICES

The Church's Ministry to Those Who Serve

O God, bless our men, women and families of the Armed Services. Visit and sustain the lives of all chaplains in their rounds, duties and deployments. Give all who serve confident hearts in their work as peacemakers and peacekeepers. Protect our nation and its people in these difficult times. Never, Lord, let us abandon the character of righteousness in everything we do. Amen.

A PRAYER BOOK
for
THE ARMED SERVICES

for Chaplains and Those in Service

2008 revised edition
Published for the Bishop Suffragan
for Federal Service (Chaplaincies)
The Episcopal Church

CHURCH PUBLISHING
an imprint of
Church Publishing Incorporated, New York

The forms for Daily Devotions, the celebration of the Sacraments, the Psalms, and many of the prayers in this book are reprinted from The Book of Common Prayer of The Episcopal Church. The corresponding material in Spanish is taken from El Libro de Oración Común, copyright © 1982 by The Church Pension Fund. Used by permission.

The Personal Prayers for Those in Harm's Way are copyright © 2006 by Jennifer Phillips. Used by permission.

Other prayers are adaptations from earlier editions of this book and from other sources.

The Bible readings are taken from the New Revised Standard Version of the Bible, copyright © 1989 by the National Council of the Churches of Christ in the U.S.A. Used by permission.

Unless otherwise indicated, the hymn texts used in this book are taken from The Hymnal 1982, copyright © 1985 by The Church Pension Fund, or from Lift Every Voice and Sing II, copyright © 1993 by The Church Pension Fund. Used by permission. The text of Hymn 26 is adapted from The Hymnal 1982 and from the Book of Worship for United States Forces, printed in 1974 by the U.S. Government Printing Office.

978-0-89869-565-6

Church Publishing Incorporated
19 East 34th Street
New York, NY 10016
www.churchpublishing.org

10 9

Contents

Preface

Greetings in the Name of Our Lord and Savior Jesus Christ!

Episcopalians as well as Anglicans all over the world hope to be a loving community of support during your service. Moreover, besides encouraging you to attend one of our chapel or church services, we commend this book to you.

This revision of *A Prayer Book for the Armed Services* is an improvement on past versions, yet it honors all the noble copies distributed to those in uniform over the years without regard to any faith background. It is my hope that it will become an easy and portable companion wherever you are. Make it your own — just as other generations have done — mark favorite selections; may it bring an increased awareness of the Holy Spirit into your life.

We acknowledge, with special gratitude, the prayerful compositions of the Reverend Jennifer Philips here, as well as the dedicated work of the Reverend Gerald J. Blackburn and Mr. Frank L. Tedeschi on this edition. Their tender care is evident.

Please know of my prayers for you,

✠ The Right Reverend George E. Packard
BISHOP SUFFRAGAN FOR FEDERAL SERVICE (CHAPLAINCIES)

Foreword

Greetings in Christ Jesus. The Episcopal Church offers you this book as part of a long tradition of ministry with those who serve our nation. We hope it will bring you the strength and comfort of a growing faith in God.

May these prayers and Scripture selections give you spiritual stamina as you face the challenges of life and national service. May the words contained here assure you that Jesus has gone before you, goes with you, and will abide wherever you go.

Know that I pray for you and your families, as do Episcopalians throughout this Church, day by day and week by week. May this devotional book open another way for Christ's living presence as you seek him through serving others. Thanks be to God for all whose lives are lost — and found — in him.

✠ The Most Reverend Katharine Jefferts Schori
PRESIDING BISHOP AND PRIMATE

The Episcopal Church Service Cross

The Episcopal Church Service Cross is a five-fold cross symbolic of the five wounds of our Lord Jesus Christ at his crucifixion. The words embossed upon it, "Christ died for you," are adapted from 2 Corinthians 5:15.

The five-fold cross was originally known as the Jerusalem Cross, incorporated in the coat-of-arms of the Latin Kingdom of Jerusalem in the twelfth century as the coat-of-arms of Godfrey de Bouillon, first ruler of that kingdom.

This cross is sometimes used as the emblem of missionary work, the large center cross representing the original Church in Jerusalem, and the smaller crosses indicating the "four corners of the earth" to which Christianity was spread through missionary endeavor.

The Service Cross was designed under the direction of Edith Weir Perry, wife of Bishop James De Wolf Perry, who was Presiding Bishop of the Episcopal Church from 1930 to 1937. The cross was first issued during World War I.

This cross is a distinct mark of an Episcopalian in the Armed Services, and it is suggested that you wear it or carry it with you at all times.

A Blessing for the Episcopal Church Service Cross

O God, who is our peace, bless *this cross* with your Holy Spirit, that *it* may be *a reminder* of your peace in all circumstances, *a reminder* of the prayers of this community, and *a sign* of the love that made us and will not let us go; through Jesus Christ our Lord. *Amen.*

On presenting each Cross

Take this cross and remember that you are a child of God. May Christ's life give you life. *Amen.*

Daily Devotions

DAILY DEVOTIONS

For hundreds of years, Christian people have lifted up their hearts to God in praise and prayer in the morning and again in the evening. The brief services which follow, taken from the Book of Common Prayer, are intended to help you share in the Church's prayer at these two times of the day. There are also forms, if you wish to use them, for prayer at noon and before going to sleep at night.

Each of these services may be used every day just as they are printed on the page. You may, however, substitute other Psalms, Readings, and Prayers for those printed in the services. A table of suggested Psalms for morning and evening is on page 17. Alternative Readings and Prayers are given on pages 18–28. One of the hymns on pages 168–186 may be used in place of "O gracious Light" on page 14. Any or all of these alternatives may be used, as desired.

When these forms are used by families, or by two or more people, the Reading and Prayer should be read by one person. Other parts may be said by all together.

For these same devotions in Spanish, see pages 29–33.

On Sundays, if you cannot attend a service of worship, it is suggested that, in addition to your daily prayers, you use the devotions suggested on page 147.

In the Morning

From Psalm 51

Open my lips, O Lord, *
   And my mouth shall proclaim your praise.
Create in me a clean heart, O God, *
   and renew a right spirit within me.
Cast me not away from your presence *
   And take not your holy Spirit from me.

Give me the joy of your saving help again *
    and sustain me with your bountiful Spirit.
Glory to the Father, and to the Son, and to the Holy Spirit: *
    as it was in the beginning, is now, and will be for ever. Amen.

A Reading

Blessed be the God and Father of our Lord Jesus Christ!
By his great mercy we have been born anew to a living hope through
the resurrection of Jesus Christ from the dead.   *1 Peter 1:3*

A period of silence may follow.

A hymn may be used. (See pages 168–186.)

The Apostles' Creed may be said. (See inside the front cover.)

Prayers may be offered for ourselves and others.

The Lord's Prayer

A Closing Prayer

Lord God, almighty and everlasting Father, you have brought us in
safety to this new day: Preserve us with your mighty power, that we
may not fall into sin, nor be overcome by adversity; and in all we
do, direct us to the fulfilling of your purpose; through Jesus Christ
our Lord. *Amen.*

At Noon

From Psalm 113

Give praise, you servants of the LORD; *
    praise the Name of the LORD.
Let the Name of the LORD be blessed, *
    from this time forth for evermore.
From the rising of the sun to its going down *
    let the Name of the LORD be praised.

The LORD is high above all nations, *
    and his glory above the heavens.
Glory to the Father, and to the Son, and to the Holy Spirit: *
    as it was in the beginning, is now, and will be for ever. Amen.

A Reading

O God, you will keep in perfect peace those whose minds are fixed
on you; for in returning and rest we shall be saved; in quietness and
trust shall be our strength.   *Isaiah 26:3; 30:15*

Prayers may be offered for ourselves and others.

The Lord's Prayer

A Closing Prayer

Blessed Savior, at this hour you hung upon the cross, stretching out
your loving arms: Grant that all the peoples of the earth may look
to you and be saved; for your mercies' sake. *Amen.*

or this

Lord Jesus Christ, you said to your apostles, "Peace I give to you;
my own peace I leave with you": Regard not our sins, but the faith
of your Church, and give to us the peace and unity of that heavenly
City, where with the Father and the Holy Spirit you live and reign,
now and for ever. *Amen.*

In the Early Evening

This devotion may be used before or after the evening meal.

O gracious Light,
pure brightness of the everliving Father in heaven,
O Jesus Christ, holy and blessed!

Now as we come to the setting of the sun,
and our eyes behold the vesper light,
we sing your praises O God: Father, Son, and Holy Spirit.

You are worthy at all times to be praised by happy voices,
O Son of God, O Giver of life,
and to be glorified through all the worlds.

One or two Psalms may be said. (See page 17.)

A Reading

It is not ourselves that we proclaim; we proclaim Christ Jesus as Lord, and ourselves as your servants, for Jesus' sake. For the same God who said, "Out of darkness let light shine," has caused his light to shine within us, to give the light of revelation — the revelation of the glory of God in the face of Jesus Christ.   *2 Corinthians 4:5–6*

A hymn may be sung or said. (See pages 168–186.)

Prayers may be offered for ourselves and others.

The Lord's Prayer

A Closing Prayer

Lord Jesus, stay with us, for evening is at hand and the day is past; be our companion in the way, kindle our hearts, and awaken hope, that we may know you as you are revealed in Scripture and the breaking of bread. Grant this for the sake of your love. *Amen.*

At the Close of Day

Psalm 134

Behold now, bless the LORD, all you servants of the LORD, *
    you that stand by night in the house of the LORD.
Lift up your hands in the holy place and bless the LORD; *
    the LORD who made heaven and earth bless you out of Zion.
Glory to the Father, and to the Son, and to the Holy Spirit: *
    as it was in the beginning, is now, and will be for ever. Amen.

A Reading

Lord, you are in the midst of us and we are called by your Name:
Do not forsake us, O Lord our God.   *Jeremiah 14:9, 22*

The following song of praise or another hymn may be said

The Song of Simeon

Lord, you now have set your servant free *
  to go in peace as you have promised;
For these eyes of mine have seen the Savior, *
  whom you have prepared for all the world to see:
A Light to enlighten the nations, *
  and the glory of your people Israel.

Prayers for ourselves and others may follow. It is appropriate that prayers of thanksgiving for the blessings of the day, and penitence for our sins, be included.

The Lord's Prayer

A Closing Prayer

Visit this place, O Lord, and drive far from it all snares of the enemy; let your holy angels dwell with us to preserve us in peace; and let your blessing be upon us always; through Jesus Christ our Lord. *Amen.*

The almighty and merciful Lord, Father, Son, and Holy Spirit, bless us and keep us. *Amen.*

A TABLE OF PSALMS

The following Psalms are appropriate for use in Daily Devotions at the times indicated. The Psalms are on pages 88–105.

	Morning	Evening
Sunday	95, 146 or 118, 150	98, 114
Monday	1, 121	46
Tuesday	63, 67	84
Wednesday	51	103
Thursday	65	85, 130
Friday	22	91, 136
In Easter Season:	95, 146	
Saturday	24, 100	23, 122
Christmas Eve		67, 100
Christmas Day	98, 150	85, 146
	These same Psalms may also be used on New Year's Eve and Day.	
Epiphany	85, 146	67, 100
Sundays in Lent	63, 98	103
Sundays of Easter	118, 150	98, 114
Ascension Day	24, 150	98, 100
All Saints' Day	98, 150	46
Other Feasts	95, 98	46 or 84
Thanksgiving Day	65	67, 100
Other National Days	98, 146	67, 100

READINGS AND PRAYERS

Any of the following Bible Readings and Prayers may be used in place of those given in the forms for Daily Devotion, pages 12–16.

Acknowledge today and take to heart that the LORD is God in heaven above and on the earth beneath; there is no other.

Deuteronomy 4:39

Do not fear, for I am with you, do not be afraid, for I am your God; I will strengthen you, I will help you, I will uphold you with my victorious right hand. *Isaiah 41:10*

Jesus said, "Come to me, all that you are weary and are carrying heavy burdens, and I will give you rest. Take my yoke upon you, and learn from me; for I am gentle and humble in heart, and you will find rest for your souls. For my yoke is easy, and my burden is light." *Matthew 11:28–30*

God so loved the world that he gave his only Son, so that everyone who believes in him may not perish but may have eternal life. Indeed, God did not send the Son into the world to condemn the world, but in order that the world might be saved through him.

John 3:16–17

Jesus said, "I am the light of the world; whoever follows me will not walk in darkness, but will have the light of life." *John 8:12*

Since we are justified by faith, we have peace with God through our Lord Jesus Christ. *Romans 5:1*

The fruit of the Spirit is love, joy, peace, patience, kindness, generosity, faithfulness, gentleness, and self-control. *Galatians 5:22–23a*

There is one body and one Spirit, just as you were called to the one hope of your calling, one Lord, one faith, one baptism, one God and Father of all, who is above all and through all and in all.

Ephesians 4:4–6

Whatever you do, in word or deed, do everything in the name of the Lord Jesus, giving thanks to God the Father through him.

Colossians 3:17

My brothers and sisters, whenever you face trials of any kind, consider it nothing but joy, because you know that the testing of your faith produces endurance; and let endurance have its full effect, so that you may be mature and complete, lacking in nothing.

James 1:2–4

God's love was revealed among us in this way: God sent his only Son into the world so that we might live through him.   *1 John 4.9*

A Reading for Fridays

I have been crucified with Christ, and it is no longer I who live, but it is Christ who lives in me. And the life I now live in the flesh I live by faith in the Son of God, who loved me and gave himself for me.

Galatians 2:20

A Morning Prayer

O God, the King eternal, whose light divides the day from the night and turns the shadow of death into the morning: Drive far from us all wrong desires, incline our hearts to keep your law, and guide our feet into the way of peace; that, having done your will with cheerfulness during the day, we may, when night comes, rejoice to give you thanks; through Jesus Christ our Lord. *Amen.*

An Evening Prayer

O God, the life of all who live, the light of the faithful, the strength of those who labor, and the repose of the dead: We thank you for the blessings of the day that is past, and humbly ask for your protection through the coming night. Bring us in safety to the morning hours; through him who died and rose again for us, your Son our Savior Jesus Christ. *Amen.*

A Prayer for Fridays

Almighty God, whose most dear Son went not up to joy but first he suffered pain, and entered not into glory before he was crucified:

Mercifully grant that we, walking in the way of the cross, may find it none other than the way of life and peace; through Jesus Christ your Son our Lord. *Amen.*

SUNDAY MORNING

Reading

Amen! Blessing and glory and wisdom and thanksgiving and honor and power and might be to our God forever and ever! Amen.

Revelation 7:12

Prayer

O God our King, by the resurrection of your Son Jesus Christ on the first day of the week, you conquered sin, put death to flight, and gave us the hope of everlasting life: Redeem all our days by this victory; forgive our sins, banish our fears, make us bold to praise you and to do your will; and steel us to wait for the consummation of your kingdom on the last great Day; through the same Jesus Christ our Lord. *Amen.*

SUNDAY EVENING

Reading

Blessed be the God and Father of our Lord Jesus Christ, the Father of mercies and the God of all consolation, who consoles us in all our affliction, so that we may be able to console those who are in any affliction.   *2 Corinthians 1:3–4a*

Prayer

Lord God, whose Son our Savior Jesus Christ triumphed over the powers of death and prepared for us our place in the new Jerusalem: Grant that we, who have this day given thanks for his resurrection, may praise you in that City of which he is the light, and where he lives and reigns for ever and ever. *Amen.*

FOR THE CHURCH YEAR

When two Readings are given, one may be used in the morning and the other in the evening. See page 187 for an explanation of the Church Year.

ADVENT

(The four weeks before Christmas)

In the wilderness prepare the way of the Lord, make straight in the desert a highway for our God.　*Isaiah 40:3*

Jesus said, "Keep awake — for you do not know when the master of the house will come, in the evening, or at midnight, or at cockcrow, or at dawn, or else he may find you asleep when he comes suddenly."

Mark 13:35–36

Prayer

Almighty God, give us grace to cast away the works of darkness, and put on the armor of light, now in the time of this mortal life in which your Son Jesus Christ came to visit us in great humility; that in the last day, when he shall come again in his glorious majesty to judge both the living and the dead, we may rise to the life immortal; through him who lives and reigns with you and the Holy Spirit, one God, now and for ever. *Amen.*

CHRISTMAS SEASON

(December 25 until January 6)

A child has been born for us, a son given to us; authority rests upon his shoulders; and he is named Wonderful Counselor, Mighty God, Everlasting Father, Prince of Peace.　*Isaiah 9:6*

See, the home of God is among mortals. He will dwell with them as their God; they will be his peoples, and God himself will be with them.　*Revelation 21:3*

For the Christmas story, see page 71, no. 11.

Prayer

Almighty God, you have given your only-begotten Son to take our nature upon him, and to be born [this day] of a pure virgin: Grant that we, who have been born again and made your children by adoption and grace, may daily be renewed by your Holy Spirit; through our Lord Jesus Christ, to whom with you and the same Spirit be honor and glory, now and for ever. *Amen.*

EPIPHANY

(January 6 through the following Saturday evening)

Arise, shine; for your light has come, and the glory of the Lord has risen upon you.   *Isaiah 60:1*

Prayer

O God, by the leading of a star you manifested your only Son to the peoples of the earth: Lead us, who know you now by faith, to your presence, where we may see your glory face to face; through Jesus Christ our Lord, who lives and reigns with you and the Holy Spirit, one God, now and for ever. *Amen.*

On Sundays after Epiphany, use the Readings and Prayers for Sundays, page 20.

LENT

(Ash Wednesday until Palm Sunday)

Rend your hearts and not your clothing. Return to the Lord, your God, for he is gracious and merciful, slow to anger, and abounding in steadfast love, and relents from punishing.   *Joel 2:13*

If we say that we have no sin, we deceive ourselves, and the truth is not in us. If we confess our sins, he who is faithful and just will forgive us our sins and cleanse us from all unrighteousness.

1 John 1:8–9

Reading for Sundays in Lent

Remember Jesus Christ, raised from the dead. The saying is sure: If we have died with him, we will also live with him; if we endure, we will also reign with him; if we deny him, he will also deny us; if we are faithless, he remains faithful — for he cannot deny himself.

2 Timothy 2:8a, 11–13

Prayer

Almighty and everlasting God, you hate nothing you have made and forgive the sins of all who are penitent: Create and make in us new and contrite hearts, that we, worthily lamenting our sins and acknowledging our wretchedness, may obtain of you, the God of all mercy, perfect remission and forgiveness; through Jesus Christ our Lord, who lives and reigns with you and the Holy Spirit, one God, for ever and ever. *Amen.*

HOLY WEEK

(Palm Sunday through Holy Saturday)

He was wounded for our transgressions, crushed for our iniquities; upon him was the punishment that made us whole, and by his bruises we are healed. All we like sheep have gone astray; we have all turned to our own way, and the Lord has laid on him the iniquity of us all.   *Isaiah 53:5–6*

Christ also suffered for sins once for all, the righteous for the unrighteous, in order to bring you to God.   *1 Peter 3:18a*

For the story of Christ's death, see page 76, no. 26.

Prayer

Almighty and everliving God, in your tender love for the human race you sent your Son our Savior Jesus Christ to take upon him our nature, and to suffer death upon the cross, giving us the example of his great humility: Mercifully grant that we may walk in the way of his suffering, and also share in his resurrection; through Jesus Christ our Lord, who lives and reigns with you and the Holy Spirit, one God, for ever and ever. *Amen.*

EASTER

(Easter Day until Ascension Day)

Thanks be to God who gives us the victory through our Lord Jesus Christ.   *1 Corinthians 15:57*

You are a chosen race, a royal priesthood, a holy nation, God's own people, in order that you may proclaim the mighty acts of him who called you out of darkness into his marvelous light.   *1 Peter 2:9*

For the Easter story, see page 77, nos. 27 and 28.

Prayer

O God, who for our redemption gave your only-begotten Son to the death of the cross, and by his glorious resurrection delivered us from the power of our enemy: Grant us so to die daily to sin, that we may evermore live with him in the joy of his resurrection; through Jesus Christ your Son our Lord, who lives and reigns with you and the Holy Spirit, one God, now and for ever. *Amen.*

ASCENSION
(Ascension Day until the Day of Pentecost)

Christ did not enter a sanctuary made by human hands, a mere copy of the true one, but he entered into heaven itself, now to appear in the presence of God on our behalf.   *Hebrews 9:24*

If you have been raised with Christ, seek the things that are above, where Christ is, seated at the right hand of God.   *Colossians 3:1*

For the story of the Ascension, see page 78, no. 30.

Prayer

Almighty God, whose blessed Son our Savior Jesus Christ ascended far above all heavens that he might fill all things: Mercifully give us faith to perceive that, according to his promise, he abides with his Church on earth, even to the end of the ages; through Jesus Christ our Lord, who lives and reigns with you and the Holy Spirit, one God, in glory everlasting. *Amen.*

THE DAY OF PENTECOST

God's love has been poured into our hearts through the Holy Spirit that has been given to us.   *Romans 5:5*

For the story of Pentecost, see page 78, no. 31.

Prayer

Almighty God, on this day you opened the way of eternal life to every race and nation by the promised gift of your Holy Spirit: Shed abroad this gift throughout the world by the preaching of the Gospel, that it may reach to the ends of the earth; through Jesus Christ our Lord, who lives and reigns with you, in the unity of the Holy Spirit, one God, for ever and ever. *Amen.*

TRINITY SUNDAY

(The first Sunday after Pentecost)

Holy, holy, holy, the Lord God the Almighty, who was and is and is to come.　　*Revelation 4:8*

Prayer

Almighty and everlasting God, you have given to us your servants grace, by the confession of a true faith, to acknowledge the glory of the eternal Trinity, and in the power of your divine Majesty to worship the Unity: Keep us steadfast in this faith and worship, and bring us at last to see you in your one and eternal glory, O Father; who with the Son and the Holy Spirit live and reign, one God, for ever and ever. *Amen.*

On other Sundays after Pentecost, use the Readings and Prayers for Sundays, page 20.

ALL SAINTS' DAY

I looked, and there was a great multitude that no one could count, from every nation, from all tribes and peoples and languages, standing before the throne and before the Lamb, robed in white, with palm branches in their hands. They cried out in a loud voice, saying, "Salvation belongs to our God who is seated on the throne, and to the Lamb!"　　*Revelation 7:9–10*

Prayer

Almighty God, you have knit together your elect in one communion and fellowship in the mystical body of your Son Christ our Lord:

Give us grace so to follow your blessed saints in all virtuous and godly living, that we may come to those ineffable joys that you have prepared for those who truly love you; through Jesus Christ our Lord, who with you and the Holy Spirit lives and reigns, one God, in glory everlasting. *Amen.*

FEASTS OF OUR LORD DURING THE YEAR

Without any doubt, the mystery of our religion is great: He was revealed in flesh, vindicated in spirit, seen by angels, proclaimed among Gentiles, believed in throughout the world, taken up in glory.

1 Timothy 3:16

The Word became flesh and lived among us, and we have seen his glory, the glory as of a father's only son, full of grace and truth.

John 1:14

Prayer

Almighty God, you have poured upon us the new light of your incarnate Word: Grant that this light, enkindled in our hearts, may shine forth in our lives; through Jesus Christ our Lord, who lives and reigns with you, in the unity of the Holy Spirit, one God, now and for ever. *Amen.*

FEASTS OF APOSTLES

Those who were baptized devoted themselves to the apostles' teaching and fellowship, to the breaking of bread and the prayers.

Acts 2:42

The gifts of Christ were that some should be apostles, some prophets, some evangelists, some pastors and teachers, to equip the saints for the work of ministry, for the building up of the body of Christ.

Ephesians 4:11–12

Prayer

Almighty God, you have built your Church upon the foundation of the apostles and prophets, Jesus Christ himself being the chief cornerstone: Grant us so to be joined together in unity of spirit by their teaching, that we may be made a holy temple acceptable to you; through Jesus Christ our Lord, who lives and reigns with you and the Holy Spirit, one God, for ever and ever. *Amen.*

OTHER SAINTS' DAYS

Give thanks to the Father, who has enabled you to share in the inheritance of the saints in the light.   *Colossians 1:12*

You are no longer strangers and aliens, but you are citizens with the saints and also members of the household of God.   *Ephesians 2:19*

Prayer

Almighty God, by your Holy Spirit you have made us one with your saints in heaven and on earth: Grant that in our earthly pilgrimage we may always be supported by this fellowship of love and prayer, and know ourselves to be surrounded by their witness to your power and mercy. We ask this for the sake of Jesus Christ, in whom all our intercessions are acceptable through the Spirit, and who lives and reigns for ever and ever. *Amen.*

or this

Almighty God, you have surrounded us with a great cloud of witnesses: Grant that we, encouraged by the good example of your servant _____, may persevere in running the race that is set before us, until at last we may with him (or her) attain to your eternal joy; through Jesus Christ, the pioneer and perfecter of our faith, who lives and reigns with you and the Holy Spirit, one God, for ever and ever. *Amen.*

NATIONAL DAYS

Give thanks to the Lord, call upon his name; make known his deeds among the nations, proclaim that his Name is exalted.   *Isaiah 12:4b*

Any of the following prayers may be used.

Lord God Almighty, in whose Name the founders of our country won liberty for themselves and for us, and lit the torch of freedom for nations then unborn: Grant that we and all the people of our land may have grace to maintain our liberties in righteousness and peace; through Jesus Christ our Lord, who lives and reigns with you and the Holy Spirit, one God, for ever and ever. *Amen.*

Lord God Almighty, you have made all the peoples of the earth for your glory, to serve you in freedom and in peace: Give to the people of our country a zeal for justice and the strength of forbearance, that we may use our liberty in accordance with your gracious will; through Jesus Christ our Lord, who lives and reigns with you and the Holy Spirit, one God, for ever and ever. *Amen.*

Almighty God, we commend to your gracious care and keeping all the men and women of our armed forces at home and abroad. Defend them day by day with your heavenly grace; strengthen them in their trials and temptations; give them courage to face the perils which beset them; and grant them a sense of your abiding presence wherever they may be; through Jesus Christ our Lord. *Amen.*

In this litany, a leader reads the prayers; the people's responses are in italics.

O Lord our Governor, bless the leaders of our land, that we may be a people at peace among ourselves and a blessing to other nations of the earth.
  Lord, keep this nation under your care.

To the President and members of the Cabinet, to Governors of States, Mayors of Cities, and to all in administrative authority, grant wisdom and grace in the exercise of their duties.
  Give grace to your servants, O Lord.

To Senators and Representatives, and those who make our laws in States, Cities, and Towns, give courage, wisdom, and foresight to provide for the needs of all our people, and to fulfill our obligations in the community of nations.
  Give grace to your servants, O Lord.

To the Judges and officers of our Courts give understanding and integrity, that human rights may be safeguarded and justice served.
  Give grace to your servants, O Lord.

And finally, teach our people to rely on your strength and to accept their responsibilities to their fellow citizens, that they may elect trustworthy leaders and make wise decisions for the well-being of our society; that we may serve you faithfully in our generation and honor your holy Name.

For yours is the kingdom, O Lord, and you are exalted
as head above all. Amen.

DEVOCIONES DIARIAS

Por la Mañana

Del Salmo 51

Señor, abre mis labios, *
    y mi boca proclamará tu alabanza.
Crea en mí, oh Dios, un corazón limpio, *
    y renueva un espíritu firme dentro de mí.
No me eches de tu presencia, *
    y no quites de mí tu santo Espíritu.
Dame otra vez el gozo de tu salvación; *
    y que tu noble Espíritu me sustente.
Gloria al Padre, y al Hijo y al Espíritu Santo: *
    como era en el principio, ahora y siempre,
    por los siglos de los siglos. Amén.

Lectura

Bendito el Dios y Padre de nuestro Señor Jesucristo, que según su grande misericordia nos hizo renacer para una esperanza viva, por la resurrección de Jesucristo de los muertos.   *1 San Pedro 1:3*

Puede seguir un período de silencio.

Puede usarse un himno o cántico.

Puede decirse el Credo de los Apóstoles.
    (Vea dentro de la cubierta frontal.)

Puede ofrecerse plegarias por nosotros mismos y por los demás.

El Padre Nuestro

Oración

Señor Dios, todopoderoso y eterno Padre, nos hiciste llegar sanos
y salvos hasta este nuevo día: Consévanos con tu gran poder, para
que no caigamos en pecado, ni no venza la adversidad; y, en todo
lo que hagamos, dirígenos a realizar tus designios; por Jesucristo
nuestro Señor. *Amén.*

Al Mediodía

Del Salmo 113

Alaben las obras del Señor; *
    alaben el Nombre del Señor.
Sea bendito el Nombre del Señor, *
    desde ahora y para siempre.
Desde el naciento del sol hasta donde se pone, *
    sea alabado el Nombre del Señor.
Excelso sobre las naciones es el Señor, *
    sobre los cielos su gloria.
Gloria al Padre, y al Hijo y al Espíritu Santo: *
    como era en el principio, ahora y siempre,
    por los siglos de los siglos. *Amén.*

Lectura

Oh Dios, tú guardarás en completa paz a aquél cuyo pensamiento
en ti persevera; porque en descanso y en reposo seremos salvos; en
quietude y en confianza será nuestra fortaleza.   *Isaías 26:3; 30:15*

Puede ofrecerse plegarias por nosotros mismos y por los demás.

El Padre Nuestro

Oración

Bendito Salvador, en esta hora colgabas en la cruz, extendiendo tus
brazos amorosos: Concede que todos los pueblos de la tierra miren
hacia ti y sean salvos; por tu entrañable misericordia. *Amén.*

o bien:

Señor Jesucristo, que dijiste a tus apóstoles, "La paz les dejo, mi paz les doy": No mires nuestros pecados sino la fe de tu Iglesia: y concédenos la paz y la unidad de esa Ciudad celestial; donde con el Padre y el Espíritu Santo tú vives y reinas ahora y por siempre. *Amén.*

Al Atardecer

Esta devoción puede usarse antes o después de la cena.

Luz alegrante,
claridad pura del sempiterno Padre celestial,
Jesucristo, santo y bendito:

Ahora que hemos llegado al ocaso del sol,
y nuestros ojos miran la luz vespertina,
te alabamos con himnos, oh Dios: Padre,
    Hijo y Espíritu Santo.

Digno eres de ser alabado en todos los tiempos
    con voces gozosas,
oh Hijo de Dios, Dador de la vida;
    por tanto te glorifica el universo entero.

Una o dos salmos pueden ser recitados. (Vea páginas 105–109.)

Lectura

No nos predicamos a nosotros mismos, sino a Jesucristo como Señor, y a nosotros como siervos de ustedes por amor de Jesús. Porque Dios, que mandó que de las tinieblas resplandeciese la luz, es el que resplandeció en nuestros corazones, para iluminación del conocimiento de la gloria de Dios en la faz de Jesucristo.

2 Corintios 4:5–6

Puede ofrecerse plegarias por nosotros mismos y por los demás.

El Padre Nuestro

Oración

Quédate con nosotros, Señor Jesús, ahora que la noche se acerca
y ha pasado el día. Sé nuestro companero en el camino, enciende
nuestros corazones, y despierta la esperanza, para que te conoz-
camos tal como te revelas en las Escrituras y en la fracción del pan.
Concede esto por amor de tu Nombre. *Amén.*

Al Terminar el Día

Salmo 134

Y ahora bendigan el Señor,
siervos todos del Señor, *
　　los que de noche están de pie en la casa del Señor.
Eleven las manos hacia el santuario,
y bendigan al Señor. *
　　El Señor que hizo los cielos y la tierra,
　　te bendiga desde Sión.

Lectura

Tú estás entre nosotros, oh Señor, y sobre nosotros es invocado tu
Nombre; no nos desampares, Señor nuestro Dios.　*Jeremías 14:9, 22*

Puede decirse lo siguiente:

Cántico de Simeón

Ahora despides, Señor, a tu siervo. *
　　conforme a tu palabra, en paz;
Porque mis ojos han visto a tu Salavador, *
　　a quien has presentato ante todos los pueblos;
Luz para alumbrar a las naciones. *
　　Y gloria de tu pueblo Israel.

*Pueden seguir plegarias por nosotros mismo y por los demás. Es apropiado
que se incluyan oraciones de acción de gracias por las bendiciones del día, y
de penitencia por nuestros pecados.*

El Padre Nuestro

Oración

Visita, oh Señor, este lugar, y ahuyenta de él todas las asechanzas del enemigo; que tus santos ángeles moren con nosotros para preservarnos en paz; y que tu bendición sea siempre sobre nosotros; por Jesucristo nuestro Señor. *Amén*.

Que el Señor omnipotente y misericordioso: Padre, Hijo y Espíritu Santo, nos bendiga y nos guarde. *Amén*.

Prayers

PRAYERS

Like most Christians, Episcopalians frequently pray in words written by other people. There are many reasons for this. One is that such prayers sometimes say what we want to say better than we can say it ourselves. Another is that they suggest topics for prayer we might not have thought of, but which we are glad to make our own. Some written prayers are very old, and have been hallowed by the lips of millions of Christians through the centuries. Others are new, and express the concerns of the world today.

It is also important that we pray in our own words. Our prayer may be very simple. It may be long or short. The important thing is that we pray in faith. Ordinarily, Christian prayer is addressed to God (the Father) through Jesus Christ, and in the power of the Holy Spirit. We may also address our prayers directly to Jesus or to the Holy Spirit.

Most of the prayers in this section follow a pattern known as the "collect" form — a prayer usually said by one person on behalf of the entire worshiping group. Many people use this same form when making up their own prayers (although this is not necessary).

Most of these prayers have the following structure:

1. *The address to God.* This may be very short, such as "O God," or it may be longer, such as "Merciful and loving God." Sometimes a phrase or clause is added to the address, such as "creator of heaven and earth" or "you are more willing to listen than we are to pray."

2. *The petition.* Here God is asked to do something for the person or persons praying or for others. Sometimes a reason for the prayer is added, such as "that all people may live in peace and safety" or "that we may love you more and serve you better."

3. *The conclusion.* This may be short, such as "we ask this through Jesus our Savior," or it may be long, such as "through Jesus Christ our Lord, who lives and reigns with you and the Holy Spirit, one God, for ever and ever. Amen."

A GUIDE TO THE PRAYERS

In the prayers that follow (and throughout this book) the italicized words "he," "him," and "his" should be changed to "she," "her," "hers," "they," "them," or "theirs" as appropriate.

Personal Prayers for Healing and Renewal

1. For Trust in God

O God, the source of all health: So fill my heart with faith in your love, that with calm expectancy I may make room for your power to possess me, and gracefully accept your healing; through Jesus Christ our Lord. Amen.

God of all comfort, our very present help in trouble, be near to me. Look on me with the eyes of your mercy; comfort me with a sense of your presence; preserve me from the enemy; and give me patience in my affliction. Restore me to health, and lead me to your eternal glory; through Jesus Christ our Lord. Amen.

2. For Sleep

O heavenly Father, you give your children sleep for the refreshing of soul and body: Grant me this gift, I pray; keep me in that perfect peace which you have promised to those whose minds are fixed on you; and give me such a sense of your presence, that in the hours of silence I may enjoy the blessed assurance of your love; through Jesus Christ our Savior. Amen.

3. In the Morning

Lord God, almighty and everlasting Father, you have brought me in safety to this new day: Preserve me with your mighty power, that I may not fall into sin, nor be overcome by adversity; and in all I do, direct me to the fulfilling of your purpose; through Jesus Christ our Lord. Amen.

4. In the Evening

Lord Jesus, stay with me, for evening is at hand and the day is past; be my companion in the way, kindle my heart, and awaken my hope, that I may know you as you are revealed in Scripture and the breaking of bread. Grant this for the sake of your love. Amen.

5. For Protection

Christ, light of light, brightness indescribable, the Wisdom, power and glory of God, the Word made flesh: you overcame the forces of Satan, redeemed the world, then ascended again to the Father. Grant me, I pray, in this tarnished world, the shining of your splendor. Send your Archangel Michael to defend me, to guard my going out and coming in, and to bring me safely to your presence, where you reign in the one, holy and undivided Trinity, to ages of ages. Amen.

6. For Recovery from Sickness

Spirit of all healing, visit me, your child; in your power, renew health within me and raise me up in joy, according to your loving-kindness, for which I give thanks and praise; through Jesus Christ our Savior. Amen.

7. For Strength and Confidence

Gracious God, only source of life and health: Help, comfort, and relieve me, and give your power of healing to those who minister to my needs; that my weakness may be turned to strength and confidence in your loving care; for the sake of Jesus Christ. Amen.

8. For Guidance

Heavenly Father, in you I live and move and have my being: I humbly pray you so to guide and govern me by your Holy Spirit, that in all the cares and occupations of this life I may not forget you, but may remember that I am ever walking in our sight; through Jesus Christ our Lord. Amen.

9. A Prayer for Guidance by Thomas Merton

My Lord God, I have no idea where I am going. I do not see the road ahead of me. I cannot know for certain where it will end. Nor do I really know myself, and the fact that I think I am following your will does not mean that I am actually doing so. But I believe that the desire to please you does in fact please you. And I hope I have that desire in all that I am doing. I hope that I will never do anything apart from that desire. And I know that if I do this you will lead me by the right road, though I may know nothing about it. Therefore I will trust you always, though I may seem to be lost and in the shadow of death. I will not fear, for you are ever with me, and you will never leave me to face my perils alone.

10. For Rest

O God, my refuge and strength: in this place of unrelenting light and noise, enfold me in your holy darkness and silence, that I may rest secure under the shadow of your wings. Amen.

11. In Times of Personal Distress

Lord Christ, you came into the world as one of us, and suffered as we do. As I go through the trials of life, help me to realize that you are with me at all times and in all things; that I have no secrets from you; and that your loving grace enfolds me for eternity. In the security of your embrace I pray. Amen.

12. For Serenity

Merciful Jesus, you are my guide, the joy of my heart, the author of my hope, and the object of my love. I come seeking refreshment and peace. Show me your mercy, relieve my fears and anxieties, and grant me a quiet mind and an expectant heart, that by the assurance of your presence I may learn to abide in you, who is my Lord and my God. Amen.

Jesus, let your mighty calmness lift me above my fears and frustrations. By your deep patience, give me tranquility and stillness of soul in you. Make me in this, and in all, more and more like you. Amen.

Personal Prayers for Those in Harm's Way

13. For Encouragement

God of surprises,
show me your grace
in those things I did not choose,
those things I would rather avoid,

those things which bring me unhappiness.
In my day of trouble,
give me a hand of comfort and friendship.
In my bleak surroundings
show me a glimpse of your glory.
In the endless hours
send me a moment of laughter and forgetfulness.
In the long labor and anxiety of war,
open a small window of blessing for me
and for each of these others who need your
light and encouraging touch. Amen.

14. For Continuing to Trust

God my Wisdom and Shield:
Do not let my trust be destroyed,
though enemies hide in concealment
and my road is beset with dangers,
though innocence is hard to discern
and I must be cautious and vigilant.
Still, keep my mind hopeful and calm
and deliver me from hatred.
Let me see goodness where it is to be found
and rejoice in friends and allies.
Let my steps this day be in safety,
my eyes open, my heart at rest in your peace. Amen.

15. For Help in Trouble

I started out so bravely
and now I'm sinking,
I'm afraid
Lord, save me!
I was so self confident, so sure,
and now I trust nothing
and do not know where to turn for help,
and so I cry out to you,
even when I'm not sure I believe in you
or in your power to rescue me.

Lord, save me!
When Peter called out to Jesus to save him from sinking,
Jesus stretched out his hand and caught him.
Stretch out your hand, Savior, to me.
Catch me and hold me fast! Amen.

16. Bowed Down By Sin

My sin is before me,
a great heap of rubble that I cannot see over.
The burden of what I have done crushes me to the ground,
fills me with grief.
And yet, God, the measure of your mercy
far surpasses all my evil;
your love for me outweighs all I have done.
And so I am lifted up,
my heart is raised from the death of sin
and set at liberty by your sheer gift of goodness.
Despite everything,
you hold out toward me your arms of life!
I give you thanks. Amen.

17. When Faith Is Shaken

Around the world
the prayer of all the faithful rises to you,
God of a thousand names and endless mercy.
In the hours when my faith is shaken,
when my way seems unsure,
when my footsteps falter,
when I have no words to pray,
let their prayers carry me along
in the tide of love and devotion
which comes from you and return to you
without ceasing.
You know what is in our hearts,
and our prayer is acceptable in your hearing.
Even when I cannot pray to you,
hear and have mercy! Amen.

18. For a Family Farewell to a Deployed Member

Into your care we place our beloved _____,
asking you to be *her* tower of safety and strength,
her comfort and refuge in danger.
Watch over *her* wherever she goes.
Stand at *her* side in battle.
Keep *her* safe from enemy and accident.
Defend *her*, waking and sleeping.
Bless *her* as she travels
and let our love be an anchor and a joy for *her*
through the time we are apart;
and then, return *her* to us in safety.
We ask this in your Holy Name. Amen.

19. Before Travel

God of surprising grace:
Meet me today along the road,
wherever my travels may take me.
Open my eyes to see you,
and let my heart burn with joy,
knowing your near presence
and your unfailing love. Amen.

20. At Bedtime

I lie down in peace, at once I fall asleep;
for only you, Lord, make me dwell in safety.
Through all the rustles and murmurs of the night,
you watch over me, so I may close my eyes.
In the dangers and uncertainties of the world,
you open for me an oasis of restful calm.
On your breast I may lay down my head,
and release the weight of the day into your care.
Into your hands I entrust my comrades and friends;
for, like me, they are precious in your sight.
Let me sleep, secure now, and when morning comes
rise up in refreshment and strength to do your will. Amen.

21. During Night Hours

In the night hours, I call to you,
God my protection and peace:
be very near to me.
As I am afraid, bear me up in courage.
As I am in weariness of heart, renew me by your Spirit.
As I miss my loved ones and home, comfort me with your presence.
For you hold the universe in love,
and not a sparrow falls without your attention.
Help me to put my trust in you
and rest securely through this night,
feeling beneath me your everlasting arms. Amen.

22. In Sleepless Night Hours

God who keeps guard over us:
through the sounds of this camp at night,
through the breathing of my comrades,
the wind, and the sounds of those at work and at watch,
I cry to you in my heart.
I need your closer presence.
Do not be far off.
Hear me and come to my aid.
Drive off all the demons of fear and worry
that trouble my sleep
and the sleep of others in this place.
When so many need your comfort and your strength, I wonder:
who am I that you should be mindful of me and love me?
But you do!
And so I thank you and give you praise. Amen.

23. For a Spouse

Blessed God, you have lifted up my heart in gladness
in the gift of _____, my *wife*.
Thank you for the warm thought of *her*
that bring me cheer and comfort far from home.
Lift up *her* heart also
with the sure knowledge of my love.

Watch over *her* going out and *her* coming in,
and keep *her* in safety and hope
until we meet again. Amen.

24. For a Loved One

God your love is better known to me
because of the love of _____,
for which I give you great thanks.
Watch over *her* and keep *her*;
encourage *her* heart,
help *her* trust in my love and in yours.
Confirm us in faithfulness,
buttress our patience,
enliven our hope,
deepen our connection,
even while we are apart.
Let our love be fortified by yours. Amen.

25. Giving Thanks for Friends

How I give you thanks and praise
for these comrades who serve beside me!
For the strength of their arms and their wills,
for their humor and grace under strain,
for their determination to watch over each other,
come what may,
God I thank you.

May I carry my share,
stand with them boldly,
guard their backs,
help bear their burdens,
treasure their confidence in me,
and be the friend to them that they have been to me,
assisted by your life-giving Spirit. Amen.

26. Thanksgiving for Comrades

Good God, I give thanks
for the courage of these brothers and sisters in arms.
For the strength of their backs and their wills,
for their grit and their trustiness,
for their spirit and determination,
for their sense and their skill,
I give you thanks.
May I be to them as good a comrade
as they have been to me,
and may your strong arm defend and empower us daily. Amen.

27. In Anxiety for Loved Ones Out of Touch in a Time of Trouble

God whose watchful eye is over all,
whose love never ceases:
give your strong help and comfort, however it might be needed
by those I love.
Stand beside them in trouble,
give them firm and hopeful hearts,
keep the knowledge of our love a wellspring of consolation
to them and to me,
and help me to hold in mind
that your Spirit of compassion and kindness
stirs many to help where others are in need.
I pray in your Holy Name. Amen.

28. Those in Command

God, our sentinel and sure defense:
I commend to your care my commanding officer _____ .
Lend *him* your wisdom and courage.
Give *him* firmness of will,
clarity and justice in deciding,
prudence and care in planning,
and a kind and fair disposition towards all in *his* charge,
safety in all *his* steps,

and a guiding sense of your presence
this day and always. Amen.

20. Flight Prayer

Taking the wings of the morning,
I give you praise.
You spread the sky like a tent over me;
you fold the mountains and stretch the deserts and seas below;
in the delight of space and speed I thank you;
even here you are with me,
lending me your wings and your sure protection.
At my flight's end give me fair weather,
a clean landing, and a welcome home. Amen.

30. Communion by Intention

Though I am far from church and sacrament,
I invite you into my heart, blessed Christ.
As I look to the horizon, I know the whole world
to be bread lifted in your sight to be made holy
according to your will;
and all the life running within it
to be your blood poured out for healing
and reconciliation.
You are host at the banquet of my life,
and every day you feed me with yourself in love.
Grant this prayer to be my Communion with you
by my intention, and desire,
to make me holy as you are holy. Amen.

31. If I forget to Pray

If there is a moment in the day to come
when I am in danger
and have no time to call on your help,
God my Defender,
be with me then.

In the instant of need,
in the flash of gratitude for trouble averted,
in the crisis of confusion,
in sudden fear,
in the moment of relief and safety,
when I forget to pray,
still hear my prayer. Amen.

32. When Moving to a New Camp

God, you led your people
as a pillar of fire by night and of cloud by day:
go before us also, as we are on the move
to a new camp.
Light our way in the darkness;
shelter us in the heat of day
and the weariness of travel;
be with us at every step and at every mile
lending us your strength for our journey,
your Spirit to lift up our hearts. Amen.

33. In a Time of Re-Deployment

Steadfast God, you led your people
through many lands and through many challenges,
and everywhere you were with them
to guard and guide them in your way.
Accompany me now in my change of duty station.
Bless to me those I leave behind
and the new comrades ahead.
Bless the work completed
and all I must leave unfinished,
and the tasks that are to come.
Lift me up in your strength
and your Spirit of hopefulness,
that I may serve faithfully
in every place
and always walk with honor in your sight. Amen.

34. For One with Troubling Memories

Deliver me, God my Peace, from the dread of memory,
from the violence that fills my eyes and has not left my heart.
Lift from me distressing dreams,
regrets, doubts, and speculations.
The past is done.
Help me to lay it in your compassionate and forgiving hands
and to trust myself and all others to your mercy.
Let gladness and ease of heart return to me,
and let me never forget that your love for me endures
even when I cannot love myself. Amen.

Six Classic Prayers for Daily Use

35. An Act of Faith

I believe and trust in God the Father
who made the world.
I believe and trust in his Son Jesus Christ
who redeemed humankind.
I believe and trust in the Holy Spirit
who gives life to the people of God.

36. Saint Patrick's Breastplate

Christ be with me, Christ within me,
Christ behind me, Christ before me,
Christ beside me, Christ to win me,
Christ to comfort and restore me,
Christ beneath me, Christ above me,
Christ in quiet, Christ in danger,
Christ in hearts of all that love me,
Christ in mouth of friend and stranger.

37. Prayer of Saint Richard of Chichester

Lord Jesus Christ, we thank you
for all the benefits you have won for us,
for all the pains and insults you have borne for us.
Most merciful redeemer, friend, and brother,

may we know you more clearly,
love you more dearly,
and follow you more nearly, day by day.

38. God Be in My Head
God be in my head, and in my understanding;
God be in my eyes, and in my looking;
God be in my mouth, and in my speaking;
God be in my heart, and in my thinking;
God be at my end, and at my departing.

39. The Jesus Prayer
Lord Jesus Christ, Son of God,
have mercy on me, a sinner.

40. A Prayer Attributed to St. Francis
Lord, make us instruments of your peace. Where there is hatred, let
us sow love; where there is injury, pardon; where there is discord,
union; where there is doubt, faith; where there is despair, hope;
where there is darkness, light; where there is sadness, joy. Grant
that we may not so much seek to be consoled as to console; to be
understood as to understand; to be loved as to love. For it is in
giving that we receive; it is in pardoning that we are pardoned; and
it is in dying that we are born to eternal life. *Amen.*

Prayers for Public Worship and Various Occasions

41. For Joy in God's Creation
O heavenly Father, you have filled the world with beauty: Open our
eyes to behold your gracious hand in all your works; that, rejoicing
in your whole creation, we may learn to serve you with gladness;
for the sake of him through whom all things were made, your Son
Jesus Christ our Lord. *Amen.*

42. For Peace
Eternal God, in whose perfect kingdom no sword is drawn but the
sword of righteousness, no strength known but the strength of love:

So mightily spread abroad your Spirit, that all peoples may be gathered under the banner of the Prince of Peace, as children of one Father; to whom be dominion and glory, now and for ever. *Amen.*

43. For Peace Among the Nations

Almighty God our heavenly Father, guide the nations of the world into the way of justice and truth, and establish among them that peace which is the fruit of righteousness, that they may become the kingdom of our Lord and Savior Jesus Christ. *Amen.*

44. For Our Enemies

O God, the Father of all, whose Son commanded us to love our enemies: Lead them and us from prejudice to truth; deliver them and us from hatred, cruelty, and revenge; and in your good time enable us all to stand reconciled before you; through Jesus Christ our Lord. *Amen.*

45. For the Unity of the Church

Almighty Father, whose blessed Son before his passion prayed for his disciples that they might be one, as you and he are one: Grant that your Church, being bound together in love and obedience to you, may be united in one body by the one Spirit, that the world may believe in him whom you have sent, your Son Jesus Christ our Lord. *Amen.*

46. For the Mission of the Church

O God, you have made of one blood all the peoples of the earth, and sent your blessed Son to preach peace to those who are far off and to those who are near: Grant that people everywhere may seek after you and find you; bring the nations into your fold; pour out your Spirit upon all flesh; and hasten the coming of your kingdom; through Jesus Christ our Lord. *Amen.*

47. For Those to Be Baptized or Confirmed

O God, you prepared your disciples for the coming of the Spirit through the teaching of your Son Jesus Christ: Make the hearts and minds of your servants ready to receive the blessing of the Holy Spirit, that they may be filled with the strength of his presence; through Jesus Christ our Lord. *Amen.*

48. For Our Country

Lord God Almighty, you have made all the peoples of the earth for your glory, to serve you in freedom and in peace: Give to the people of our country a zeal for justice and the strength of forbearance, that we may use our liberty in accordance with your gracious will; through Jesus Christ our Lord. *Amen.*

Lord God Almighty, in whose Name the founders of this country won liberty for themselves and for us, and lit the torch of freedom for nations then unborn: Grant that we and all the people of this land may have grace to maintain our liberties in righteousness and peace; through Jesus Christ our Lord, who lives and reigns with you and the Holy Spirit, one God, for ever and ever. *Amen.*

49. For the President

O Lord, whose glory is in all the world: We commend this nation to your merciful care, that, being guided by your Providence, we may dwell secure in your peace. Grant to the President of the United States, and to all in authority, wisdom and strength to know and to do your will. Fill them with the love of truth and righteousness, and make them ever mindful of their calling to serve this people in your fear; through Jesus Christ our Lord. *Amen.*

50. For the Armed Forces

Almighty God, we commend to your gracious care and keeping all the men and women of our armed forces at home and abroad. Defend them day by day with your heavenly grace; strengthen them in their trials and temptations; give them courage to face the perils which beset them; and grant them a sense of your abiding presence wherever they may be; through Jesus Christ our Lord. *Amen.*

51. For Social Justice

Almighty God, who created us in your own image: Grant us grace fearlessly to contend against evil and to make no peace with oppression; and, that we may reverently use our freedom, help us to employ it in the maintenance of justice in our communities and among the nations, to the glory of your holy Name; through Jesus Christ our Lord. *Amen.*

52. For the Poor and the Neglected

Almighty and most merciful God, we remember before you all poor and neglected persons whom it would be easy for us to forget: the homeless and the destitute, the old and the sick, and all who have none to care for them. Help us to heal those who are broken in body or spirit, and to turn their sorrow into joy. Grant this, Father, for the love of your Son, who for our sake became poor, Jesus Christ our Lord. *Amen.*

53. For the Hungry

Eternal God, who fed your people with manna in the wilderness: Look with pity on all those who today are hungry. Open our hearts and hands to help them, and inspire the leaders of the world to work for the welfare of all the people; through Jesus Christ our Lord. *Amen.*

54. For Prisoners

We beseech you, O God, for all prisoners and captives, and for all who suffer from oppression. Show them your mercy and love, we pray, and make the hearts of human beings as merciful as your own; through Jesus Christ our Lord. *Amen.*

55. For the Right Use of God's Gifts

Almighty God, whose loving hand has given us all that we possess: Grant us grace that we may honor you with our substance, and, remembering the account which we must one day give, may be faithful stewards of your bounty, through Jesus Christ our Lord. *Amen.*

Almighty and gracious Father, we give you thanks for the fruits of the earth in their season and for the labors of those who harvest them. Make us, we pray, faithful stewards of your great bounty, for the provision of our necessities and the relief of all who are in need, to the glory of your Name; through Jesus Christ our Lord, who lives and reigns with you and the Holy Spirit, one God, now and for ever. *Amen.*

56. For Married Persons

O gracious and everliving God, you have created us male and female in your image: Look mercifully upon _____ and _____ (*or all married persons*), and assist them with your grace, that with true fidelity and steadfast love they may honor and keep the promises and vows they have made to each other; through Jesus Christ our Lord. *Amen.*

57. For Those Who Live Alone

Almighty God, whose Son had nowhere to lay his head: Grant that those who live alone may not be lonely in their solitude, but that, following in his steps, they may find fulfillment in loving you and their neighbors; through Jesus Christ our Lord. *Amen.*

58. For the Care of Children

Almighty God, heavenly Father, you have blessed us with the joy and care of children: Give us calm strength and patient wisdom as we bring them up, that we may teach them to love whatever is just and true and good, following the example of our Savior Jesus Christ. *Amen.*

59. For Young Persons

God our Father, you see your children growing up in an unsteady and confusing world: Show them that your ways give more life than the ways of the world, and that following you is better than chasing after selfish goals. Help them to take failure, not as a measure of their worth, but as a chance for a new start. Give them strength to hold their faith in you, and to keep alive their joy in your creation; through Jesus Christ our Lord. *Amen.*

60. For a Birthday

O God, our times are in your hand: Look with favor, we pray, on your servant _____ as *he* begins another year. Grant that *he* may grow in wisdom and grace, and strengthen *his* trust in your goodness all the days of *his* life; through Jesus Christ our Lord. *Amen.*

61. For the Absent

O God, whose fatherly care reaches to the uttermost parts of the earth: We humbly beseech you graciously to behold and bless those whom we love, now absent from us. Defend them from all dangers of soul and body; and grant that both they and we, drawing nearer to you, may be bound together by your love in the communion of your Holy Spirit, and in the fellowship of your saints; through Jesus Christ our Lord. *Amen.*

62. For Those We Love

Almighty God, we entrust all who are dear to us to your never-failing care and love, for this life and the life to come, knowing that you are doing for them better things than we can desire or pray for; through Jesus Christ our Lord. *Amen.*

63. For a Person in Trouble

O merciful God, you have taught us in your holy Word that you desire good things for all your children: Look with pity upon your servant _____ in *his* time of trouble. Remember *him*, O Lord, in mercy, nourish *his* soul with patience, comfort *him* with a sense of your goodness, let your blessing be upon *him*, and give *him* peace; through Jesus Christ our Lord. *Amen.*

64. For the Victims of Addiction

O blessed Lord, you ministered to all who came to you: Look with compassion upon all who through addiction have lost their health and freedom. Restore to them the assurance of your unfailing mercy; remove from them the fears that beset them; strengthen them in the work of their recovery; and to those who care for them, give patient understanding and persevering love. *Amen.*

65. For the Wounded

Have mercy, O God, on all those who today are wounded and suffering. Since their families and friends are far away, let your grace be their comfort. Raise them to health again, if that is your will for them, but chiefly give them patience and faith in you; through Jesus Christ our Lord. *Amen.*

66. For Sick or Wounded Persons

O Lord, look down from heaven: Behold, visit, and relieve your *servants* _____ . Look upon *them* with the eyes of your mercy, give *them* comfort and sure confidence in you, defend *them* in all danger, and keep *them* in perpetual peace and safety; through Jesus Christ our Lord. *Amen.*

67. A Jewish Prayer on Behalf of the Sick

O Lord God, you are gracious and merciful; you spread your wings of protection and tender care over all your creatures; you heal the sick and bind up their wounds. Receive, we beseech you, our humble petition on behalf of _____ who is confined to the bed of pain and sickness. Send *him,* O God, your healing, that *he* may speedily recover from the illness that has come upon *him.* Sustain *his* spirit, relieve *his* pain, and restore *him* to perfect health, happiness, and usefulness. Instill into *his* impaired body the balm of Gilead that *he* may be able to bear testimony to your everlasting mercy and love, for you, O Lord, are a faithful and merciful healer. *Amen.*

68. For Recovery from Sickness

O God, the strength of the weak and the comfort of sufferers: Mercifully accept our prayers, and grant to your servant _____ the help of your power, that *his* sickness may be turned into health, and our sorrow into joy; through Jesus Christ our Lord. *Amen.*

69. For a Sick Child

Heavenly Father, watch with us over your child _____, and grant that *he* may be restored to that perfect health which it is yours alone to give; through Jesus Christ our Lord. *Amen.*

70. Prayers for Use by a Sick Person

O Father of mercies and God of all comfort: Look upon me and stay with me in this time of weakness and pain. Strengthen my soul and my body, and drive away from me all fear, depression, resentment, and every other bitter mood or evil thought. Bless the doctors, nurses, medics, and all others who are helping me to stay alive and to recover. Help me to cooperate with them patiently and cheerfully. Grant that in time I may be healed, and that I may not forget your goodness to me. Finally, O God, have mercy on those whose suffering is worse than my own. I ask all this through Jesus Christ my Savior. *Amen.*

Lord Jesus Christ, by your patience in suffering you hallowed earthly pain and gave us the example of obedience to your Father's will: Be near me in my time of weakness and pain; sustain me by your grace, that my strength and courage may not fail; heal me according to your will; and help me always to believe that what happens to me here is of little account if you hold me in eternal life, my Lord and my God. *Amen.*

71. Prayers for the Departed

O God, who by the glorious resurrection of your Son Jesus Christ destroyed death, and brought life and immortality to light: Grant that your servant _____, being raised with him, may know the strength of his presence, and rejoice in his eternal glory; who with you and the Holy Spirit lives and reigns, one God, for ever and ever. *Amen.*

O God, whose mercies cannot be numbered: Accept our prayers on behalf of your servant _____, and grant *him* an entrance into the land of light and joy, in the fellowship of your saints; through Jesus Christ our Lord. *Amen.*

O God of grace and glory, we remember before you this day our brother (sister) _____ . We thank you for giving *him* to us, *his* [family and] friends, to know and to love as a companion on our earthly pilgrimage. In your boundless compassion, console us who mourn. Give us faith to see in death the gate of eternal life, so that in quiet confidence we may continue our course on earth, until, by your call, we are reunited with those who have gone before; through Jesus Christ our Lord. *Amen.*

72. For Those Who Have Given Their Lives

Almighty God, our heavenly Father, in whose hands are the living and the dead: We give you thanks for all your servants who have laid down their lives in the service of their country. Grant to them your mercy and the light of your presence; and give us such a lively sense of your righteous will, that the work which you have begun in them may be perfected; through Jesus Christ your Son our Lord. *Amen.*

73. For Those who Mourn

Almighty God, Father of mercies and giver of comfort: Deal graciously, we pray, with all who mourn; that, casting all their care on you they may know the consolation of your love; through Jesus Christ our Lord. *Amen.*

74. For Quiet Confidence

O God of peace, you have taught us that in returning and rest we shall be saved, in quietness and in confidence shall be our strength: By the might of your Spirit lift us, we pray you, to your presence, where we may be still and know that you are God; through Jesus Christ our Lord. *Amen.*

75. A Prayer of Self-Dedication

Almighty and eternal God, so draw our hearts to you, so guide our minds, so fill our imaginations, so control our wills, that we may be wholly yours, utterly dedicated to you; and then use us, we pray you, as you will, and always to your glory and the welfare of your people; through our Lord and Savior Jesus Christ. *Amen.*

76. Before Receiving Communion

Be present, be present, O Jesus, our great High Priest, as you were present with your disciples, and be known to us in the breaking of bread. *Amen.*

77. After Receiving Communion

God our Father, whose Son our Lord Jesus Christ in a wonderful Sacrament has left us a memorial of his passion: Grant us so to venerate the sacred mysteries of his Body and Blood, that we may ever perceive within ourselves the fruit of his redemption; who lives and reigns with you and the Holy Spirit, one God, for ever and ever. *Amen.*

78. Grace at Meals

Bless, O Lord, your gifts to our use and us to your service; for Christ's sake. *Amen.*

For these and all his mercies, God's holy Name be blessed and praised: through Jesus Christ our Lord. *Amen.*

79. The General Thanksgiving

Almighty God, Father of all mercies, we your unworthy servants give you humble thanks for all your goodness and loving-kindness to us and to all whom you have made. We bless you for our creation, preservation, and all the blessings of this life; but above all for your immeasurable love in the redemption of the world by our Lord Jesus Christ; for the means of grace, and for the hope of glory. And, we pray, give us such an awareness of your mercies, that with truly thankful hearts we may show forth your praise, not only with our lips, but in our lives, by giving up our selves to your service, and by walking before you in holiness and righteousness all our days; through Jesus Christ our Lord, to whom, with you and the Holy Spirit, be honor and glory throughout all ages. *Amen.*

80. A Thanksgiving for the Saints

O God, the King of saints, we praise and glorify your holy Name for all your servants who have finished their course in your faith and fear: for the blessed Virgin Mary; for the holy patriarchs, prophets, apostles, and martyrs; and for all your other righteous servants, known to us and unknown; and we pray that, encouraged by their examples, aided by their prayers, and strengthened by their fellowship, we also may be partakers of the inheritance of the saints in light; through the merits of your Son Jesus Christ our Lord. *Amen.*

81. Blessings

May the God of hope fill us with all joy and peace in believing through the power of the Holy Spirit. *Amen.*

Glory to God whose power, working in us, can do infinitely more than we can ask or imagine: Glory to him from generation to generation in the Church, and in Christ Jesus for ever and ever. *Amen.*

The Lord bless us and keep us. The Lord make his face to shine upon us and be gracious to us. The Lord lift up his countenance upon us and give us peace. *Amen.*

ORACIONES

82. Oración de San Francisco de Asís

Señor, haznos instrumentos de tu paz. Donde haya odio, sembremos amor; donde haya ofensa, perdón; donde haya discordia, unión; donde haya duda, fe; donde haya desesperación, esperanza; donde haya tinieblas, luz; donde haya tristeza, gozo. Concede que no busquemos ser consolados, sino consolar; ser comprendidos, sino comprender; ser amados, sino amar. Porque dando, es como recibimos; perdonando, es como somos perdonados; y muriendo, es como nacemos a la vida eterna. *Amén.*

83. Antes de Comulgar

¡Hazte presente! Hazte presente, oh Jesús, nuestro gran Sumo Sacerdote, así como te hiciste presente con tus discípulos, y muéstrate a nosotros en la fracción del Pan; tú que vives y reinas con el Padre y Espíritu Santo, ahora y por siempre. *Amén.*

84. Después de Comulgar

Oh Señor Jesucristo, que en un Sacramento maravilloso nos has dejado el memorial de tu pasión: Concédenos, te suplicamos, que de tal modo veneremos los sagrados misterios de tu Cuerpo y Sangre, que discernamos constantemente en nosotros el fruto de tu redención; tú que vives y reinas con el Padre y el Espíritu Santo, un solo Dios, por los siglos de los siglos. *Amén.*

85. Acción de Gracias por los Alimentos

Bendice, oh Señor, estos tus dones para nuestro uso, y a nosotros en tu servicio; por amor de Cristo. *Amén.*

86. Acción de Gracias por los Santos

Oh Dios, Rey de los santos, alabamos y glorificamos tu santo Nombre por todos tus siervos que han terminado su carrera en tu fe y temor: por la bendita Virgen María; por los santos patriarcas, profetas, apóstoles y mártires; y por todos tus demás siervos justos, tanto conocidos como desconocidos; y te rogamos que nosotros, estimulados por su ejemplo, ayudados por sus oraciones y fortalecidos por su comunión seamos también participes de la herencia de los santos en luz; por los méritos de tu Hijo Jesucristo nuestro Señor. *Amén.*

87. Bendiciones

Gloria a Dios, cuyo poder, actuando en nosotros, puede realizar todas las cosas infinitamente mejor de lo que podemos pedir o pensar: Gloria a El en la Iglesia de generación en generación y en Cristo Jesús por siglos de los siglos. *Amén.*

Que el Dios de la esperanza nos colme de todo gozo y paz en nuestra fe, por el poder del Espíritu Santo. *Amén.*

La gracia de nuestro Señor Jesucristo, el amor de Dios y la comunión del Espíritu Santo sean con todos nosotros, ahora y siempre. *Amén.*

Bible Readings

BIBLE READINGS

The readings given here are intended primarily for private devotion. They have been selected to help you understand more fully the wonderful things that God has done for us and for our salvation.

When meditating on Scripture, it is helpful to (1) ask God to open your heart to hear his word, (2) read the passage slowly, stopping whenever you want to think about what is being said, (3) resolve to practice in your life what you have learned from the reading, and (4) thank God for what he has taught you and pray for help to live by that teaching.

Because of the size of this book, only a few readings from the Old Testament could be included. As background to these stories, you may want to read the following passages from a Bible: Genesis, chapters 1, 6, 7, 8, 15; Exodus, chapters 2, 3, 12, 14, 19, 20; 1 Kings 8; 2 Kings 17; 2 Chronicles 36; Ezra 3; Isaiah 55.

A PRAYER FOR UNDERSTANDING HOLY SCRIPTURE

Blessed Lord, who caused all holy Scriptures to be written for our learning: Grant us so to hear them, read, mark, learn, and inwardly digest them, that we may embrace and ever hold fast the blessed hope of everlasting life, which you have given us in our Savior Jesus Christ; who lives and reigns with you and the Holy Spirit, one God, for ever and ever. Amen.

A GUIDE TO THE BIBLE READINGS

FOR THE CHURCH YEAR

Advent 9, 13, 23, 42
Christmas 10, 11
Epiphany 10, 12
Sundays after Epiphany 1, 12, 13, 14, 17, 19, 34, 35, 39
Lent 2, 3, 4, 5, 7, 8, 15, 16, 20, 25, 26, 36
Good Friday 26
Easter Season 27, 28, 21, 24, 40, 41, 42
Ascension Day 29, 30
The Day of Pentecost 5, 31
Trinity Sunday, 1, 29
Other Sundays after Pentecost *Any reading may be chosen*
Saint's Days and Other Feasts 14, 23, 29, 40, 41, 43
National Days 3, 14, 22

FOR PARTICULAR NEEDS

Baptism and Confirmation 4, 5, 8, 12, 13, 14, 19, 29, 32
Burial and Memorial Services 20, 21, 24, 40, 41, 43
The Christian Hope 20, 24, 37, 39, 40, 41, 42
In Emergencies: see pages 124, 166
Holy Communion, Preparation for 6, 14, 20, 22, 25, 33, 36
Marriage 1, 14, 18, 19, 35, 36
Repentance and Forgiveness 8, 15, 28, 32, 36, 38, 39
Sickness 16, 39, 40

1. God creates the universe and the human race

In the beginning when God created the heavens and the earth, the earth was a formless void and darkness covered the face of the deep, while a wind from God swept over the face of the waters.

Then God said, "Let there be light"; and there was light. And God saw that the light was good; and God separated the light from the darkness. God called the light Day, and the darkness he called Night. And there was evening and there was morning, the first day.

And on the sixth day God said, "Let us make humankind in our image, according to our likeness; and let them have dominion over the fish of the sea, and over the birds of the air, and over the cattle, and over all the wild animals of the earth, and over every creeping thing that creeps upon the earth." So God created humankind in his image, in the image of God he created them; male and female he created them. God blessed them, and God said to them, "Be fruitful and multiply, and fill the earth and subdue it; and have dominion over the fish of the sea and over the birds of the air and over every living thing that moves upon the earth. And to every beast of the earth, and to every bird of the air, and to everything that creeps on the earth, everything that has the breath of life, I have given every green plant for food." And it was so. God saw everything that he had made, and indeed, it was very good. *Genesis 1:1–5, 26–28a, 30b–31a*

2. The human race becomes corrupt

They heard the sound of the Lord God walking in the garden at the time of the evening breeze, and the man and his wife hid themselves from the presence of the Lord God among the trees of the garden. But the Lord God called to the man, and said to him, "Where are you?" He said, "I heard the sound of you in the garden, and I was afraid, because I was naked; and I hid myself."

He said, "Who told you that you were naked? Have you eaten from the tree of which I commanded you not to eat?" The man said, "The woman whom you gave to be with me, she gave me fruit from the tree, and I ate." Then the Lord God said to the woman, "What is this that you have done?" The woman said, "The serpent tricked me, and I ate."

The Lord God said to the serpent, "Because you have done this, cursed are you among all animals and among all wild creatures; upon your belly you shall go, and dust you shall eat all the days of your life. I will put enmity between you and the woman, and between your offspring and hers; he will strike your head, and you will strike his heel."

To the woman he said, "I will greatly increase your pangs in childbearing; in pain you shall bring forth children, yet your desire shall be for your husband, and he shall rule over you."

And to the man he said, "Because you have listened to the voice of your wife, and have eaten of the tree about which I commanded you, 'You shall not eat of it,' cursed is the ground because of you; in toil you shall eat of it all the days of your life; thorns and thistles it shall bring forth for you; and you shall eat the plants of the field. By the sweat of your face you shall eat bread until you return to the ground, for out of it you were taken; you are dust, and to dust you shall return." *Genesis 3:8–19*

3. God makes a promise to Abraham

When Abram was ninety-nine years old, the Lord appeared to Abram, and said to him, "I am God Almighty; walk before me, and be blameless. And I will make my covenant between me and you, and will make you exceedingly numerous." Then Abram fell on his face; and God said to him, "As for me, this is my covenant with you: You shall be the ancestor of a multitude of nations. No longer shall your name be Abram, but your name shall be Abraham; for I have made you the ancestor of a multitude of nations. I will make you exceedingly fruitful; and I will make nations of you, and kings shall come from you. I will establish my covenant between me and you, and your offspring after you throughout their generations, for an everlasting covenant, to be God to you and to your offspring after you. And I will give to you, and to your offspring after you, the land where you are now an alien, all the land of Canaan, for a perpetual holding; and I will be their God." *Genesis 17:1–8*

4. God rescues the Children of Israel

At the morning watch the Lord in the pillar of fire and cloud looked down upon the Egyptian army, and threw the Egyptian army into panic. He clogged their chariot wheels so that they turned with difficulty. The Egyptians said, "Let us flee from the Israelites, for the Lord is fighting for them against Egypt." Then the Lord said to Moses, "Stretch out your hand over the sea, so that the water may come back upon the Egyptians, upon their chariots and chariot drivers." So Moses stretched out his hand over the sea, and at dawn the sea returned to its normal depth. As the Egyptians fled before it, the Lord tossed the Egyptians into the sea. The waters returned and covered the chariots and the chariot drivers, the entire army of Pharaoh that had followed them into the sea; not one of them remained. But the Israelites walked on dry ground through the sea, the waters forming a wall for them on their right and on their left.

Thus the Lord saved Israel that day from the Egyptians; and Israel saw the Egyptians dead on the seashore. Israel saw the great work that the Lord did against the Egyptians. So the people feared the Lord and believed in the Lord and in his servant Moses.

Exodus 14:24–31

5. God makes a covenant with Israel

On the third new moon after the Israelites had gone out of the land of Egypt, on that very day, they came into the wilderness of Sinai. Then Moses went up to God; the Lord called to him from the mountain, saying, "Thus you shall say to the house of Jacob, and tell the Israelites: You have seen what I did to the Egyptians, and how I bore you on eagles' wings and brought you to myself. Now therefore, if you obey my voice and keep my covenant, you shall be my treasured possession out of all the peoples. Indeed, the whole earth is mine, but you shall be for me a priestly kingdom and a holy nation. These are the words that you shall speak to the Israelites."

So Moses came, summoned the elders of the people, and set before them all these words that the Lord had commanded him. The people all answered as one: "Everything that the Lord has spoken we will do." Moses reported the words of the people to the Lord.

Exodus 19:1, 3–8a

6. God gives Israel the Ten Commandments

See pages 148–149.

7. Israel is taken into exile

All the leading priests and the people also were exceedingly unfaithful, following all the abominations of the nations; and they polluted the house of the Lord that he had consecrated in Jerusalem.

The Lord, the God of their ancestors, sent persistently to them by his messengers, because he had compassion on his people and on his dwelling place; but they kept mocking the messengers of God, despising his words, and scoffing at his prophets, until the wrath of the Lord against his people became so great that there was no remedy.

Therefore he brought up against them the king of the Chaldeans, who killed their youths with the sword in the house of their sanctuary, and had no compassion on young man or young woman, the aged or the feeble; he gave them all into his hand. They burned the house of God, broke down the wall of Jerusalem, burned all its palaces with fire, and destroyed all its precious vessels. He took into exile in Babylon those who had escaped from the sword, and they became servants to him and to his sons until the establishment of the kingdom of Persia, to fulfill the word of the Lord by the mouth of Jeremiah, until the land had made up for its sabbaths. All the days that it lay desolate it kept sabbath, to fulfill seventy years.

2 Chronicles 36:14–17, 19–21

8. God promises a new covenant

The days are surely coming, says the Lord, when I will make a new covenant with the house of Israel and the house of Judah. It will not be like the covenant that I made with their ancestors when I took them by the hand to bring them out of the land of Egypt — a covenant that they broke, though I was their husband, says the

Lord. But this is the covenant that I will make with the house of Israel after those days, says the Lord: I will put my law within them, and I will write it on their hearts; and I will be their God, and they shall be my people. No longer shall they teach one another, or say to each other, "Know the Lord," for they shall all know me, from the least of them to the greatest, says the Lord; for I will forgive their iniquity, and remember their sin no more.   *Jeremiah 31:31–34*

9. *"Prepare the way of the Lord"*

Comfort, O comfort my people, says your God. Speak tenderly to Jerusalem, and cry to her that she has served her term, that her penalty is paid, that she has received from the Lord's hand double for all her sins.

A voice cries out: "In the wilderness prepare the way of the Lord, make straight in the desert a highway for our God. Every valley shall be lifted up, and every mountain and hill be made low; the uneven ground shall become level, and the rough places a plain. Then the glory of the Lord shall be revealed, and all people shall see it together, for the mouth of the Lord has spoken."

Get you up to a high mountain, O Zion, herald of good tidings; lift up your voice with strength, O Jerusalem, herald of good tidings, lift it up, do not fear; say to the cities of Judah, "Here is your God!" See, the Lord God comes with might, and his arm rules for him; his reward is with him, and his recompense before him. He will feed his flock like a shepherd; he will gather the lambs in his arms, and carry them in his bosom, and gently lead the mother sheep.

Isaiah 40:1–5, 9–11

10. *Prophecy of the Messianic King*

The people who walked in darkness have seen a great light; those who lived in a land of deep darkness — on them light has shined. For a child has been born for us, a son given to us; authority rests upon his shoulders; and he is named Wonderful Counselor, Mighty God, Everlasting Father, Prince of Peace. His authority shall grow continually, and there shall be endless peace for the throne of David and his kingdom. He will establish and uphold it with justice and with righteousness from this time onward and forevermore. The zeal of the Lord of hosts will do this.   *Isaiah 9:2, 6–7*

11. Jesus Christ is born

In those days a decree went out from Emperor Augustus that all the world should be registered. This was the first registration and was taken while Quirinius was governor of Syria. All went to their own towns to be registered. Joseph also went from the town of Nazareth in Galilee to Judea, to the city of David called Bethlehem, because he was descended from the house and family of David. He went to be registered with Mary, to whom he was engaged and who was expecting a child. While they were there, the time came for her to deliver her child. And she gave birth to her firstborn son and wrapped him in bands of cloth, and laid him in a manger, because there was no place for them in the inn.

In that region there were shepherds living in the fields, keeping watch over their flock by night. Then an angel of the Lord stood before them, and the glory of the Lord shone around them, and they were terrified. But the angel said to them, "Do not be afraid; for see — I am bringing you good news of great joy for all the people: to you is born this day in the city of David a Savior, who is the Messiah, the Lord. This will be a sign for you: you will find a child wrapped in bands of cloth and lying in a manger." And suddenly there was with the angel a multitude of the heavenly host, praising God and saying, "Glory to God in the highest heaven, and on earth peace among those whom he favors!"   *Luke 2:1–14*

12. Jesus is baptized

In those days Jesus came from Nazareth of Galilee and was baptized by John in the Jordan. And just as he was coming up out of the water, he saw the heavens torn apart and the Spirit descending like a dove on him. And a voice came from heaven, "You are my Son, the Beloved; with you I am well pleased."   *Mark 1:9–11*

13. Jesus preaches in the synagogue

When Jesus came to Nazareth, where he had been brought up, he went to the synagogue on the sabbath day, as was his custom. He stood up to read, and the scroll of the prophet Isaiah was given to him. He unrolled the scroll and found the place where it was written: "The Spirit of the Lord is upon me, because he has anointed me to bring good news to the poor. He has sent me to proclaim release to the captives and recovery of sight to the blind, to let the oppressed go free, to proclaim the year of the Lord's favor." And he rolled up the scroll, gave it back to the attendant, and sat down. The eyes of all in the synagogue were fixed on him. Then he began to say to them, "Today this scripture has been fulfilled in your hearing."

Luke 4:16–21

14. Christ teaches the Beatitudes

When Jesus saw the crowds, he went up the mountain; and after he sat down, his disciples came to him. Then he began to speak, and taught them, saying:

"Blessed are the poor in spirit, for theirs is the kingdom of heaven.
"Blessed are those who mourn, for they will be comforted.
"Blessed are the meek, for they will inherit the earth.
"Blessed are those who hunger and thirst for righteousness,
    for they will be filled.
"Blessed are the merciful, for they will receive mercy.
"Blessed are the pure in heart, for they will see God.
"Blessed are the peacemakers, for they will be called children
    of God.
"Blessed are those who are persecuted for righteousness' sake,
    for theirs is the kingdom of heaven.
"Blessed are you when people revile you and persecute you and utter all kinds of evil against you falsely on my account. Rejoice and be glad, for your reward is great in heaven, for in the same way they persecuted the prophets who were before you." *Matthew 5:1–12*

15. Christ calls sinners

Levi the tax collector gave a great banquet for him in his house; and there was a large crowd of tax collectors and others sitting at the table with them. The Pharisees and their scribes were complaining to his disciples, saying, "Why do you eat and drink with tax collectors and sinners?" Jesus answered, "Those who are well have no need of a physician, but those who are sick; I have come to call not the righteous but sinners to repentance." *Luke 5:29–32*

16. Christ heals the sick

A leader of the synagogue came in and knelt before Jesus, saying, "My daughter has just died; but come and lay your hand on her, and she will live." And Jesus got up and followed him, with his disciples. Then suddenly a woman who had been suffering from hemorrhages for twelve years came up behind him and touched the fringe of his cloak, for she said to herself, "If I only touch his cloak, I will be made well." Jesus turned, and seeing her he said, "Take heart, daughter; your faith has made you well." And instantly the woman was made well. When Jesus came to the leader's house and saw the flute players and the crowd making a commotion, he said, "Go away; for the girl is not dead but sleeping." And they laughed at him. But when the crowd had been put outside, he went in and took her by the hand, and the girl got up. And the report of this spread throughout that district. *Matthew 9:18–26*

17. Christ's true family

Jesus' mother and his brothers came to his home; and standing out-side, they sent to him and called him. A crowd was sitting around him; and they said to him, "Your mother and your brothers and sisters are outside, asking for you." And he replied, "Who are my mother and my brothers?" And looking at those who sat around him, he said, "Here are my mother and my brothers! Whoever does the will of God is my brother and sister and mother." *Mark 3:31 35*

18. Christ's teaching on marriage

Jesus said, "From the beginning of creation, 'God made them male and female.' 'For this reason a man shall leave his father and mother and be joined to his wife, and the two shall become one flesh.' So they are no longer two, but one flesh. Therefore what God has joined together, let no one separate." *Mark 10:6–9*

19. Christ welcomes children

People were bringing little children to Jesus in order that he might touch them; and the disciples spoke sternly to them. But when Jesus saw this, he was indignant and said to them, "Let the little children come to me; do not stop them; for it is to such as these that the kingdom of God belongs. Truly I tell you, whoever does not receive the kingdom of God as a little child will never enter it." And he took them up in his arms, laid his hands on them, and blessed them.

Mark 10:13–16

20. Christ is our food

Jesus said, "I am the bread of life. Whoever comes to me will never be hungry, and whoever believes in me will never be thirsty. Those who eat my flesh and drink my blood have eternal life, and I will raise them up on the last day; for my flesh is true food and my blood is true drink. Those who eat my flesh and drink my blood abide in me, and I in them. Just as the living Father sent me, and I live because of the Father, so whoever eats me will live because of me. This is the bread that came down from heaven, not like that which your ancestors ate, and they died. But the one who eats this bread will live forever." *John 6:35, 54–58*

21. The good shepherd

Jesus said, "I am the gate. Whoever enters by me will be saved, and will come in and go out and find pasture. The thief comes only to steal and kill and destroy. I came that they may have life, and have it abundantly. I am the good shepherd. The good shepherd lays down his life for the sheep. The hired hand, who is not the shepherd and does not own the sheep, sees the wolf coming and leaves the sheep and runs away — and the wolf snatches them and scatters them. The hired hand runs away because a hired hand does not care for the sheep. I am the good shepherd. I know my own and my own know me, just as the Father knows me and I know the Father. And I lay down my life for the sheep. I have other sheep that do not belong to this fold. I must bring them also, and they will listen to my voice. So there will be one flock, one shepherd."   *John 10:9 16*

22. Christ's summary of the Law

See pages 148 and 149.

23. Serving Christ in others

Jesus, sitting on the Mount of Olives, said to his disciples, "The king will say to those at his right hand, 'Come, you that are blessed by my Father, inherit the kingdom prepared for you from the foundation of the world; for I was hungry and you gave me food, I was thirsty and you gave me something to drink, I was a stranger and you welcomed me, I was naked and you gave me clothing, I was sick and you took care of me, I was in prison and you visited me.' Then the righteous will answer him, 'Lord, when was it that we saw you hungry and gave you food, or thirsty and gave you something to drink? And when was it that we saw you a stranger and welcomed you, or naked and gave you clothing? And when was it that we saw you sick or in prison and visited you?' And the king will answer them, 'Truly I tell you, just as you did it to one of the least of these who are members of my family, you did it to me.' "   *Matthew 25:34–40*

24. Christ's promise to us

Jesus said to the disciples, "Do not let your hearts be troubled. Believe in God, believe also in me. In my Father's house there are many dwelling places. If it were not so, would I have told you that I go to prepare a place for you? And if I go and prepare a place for you, I will come again and will take you to myself, so that where I am, there you may be also. And you know the way to the place where I am going." Thomas said to him, "Lord, we do not know where you are going. How can we know the way?" Jesus said to him, "I am the way, and the truth, and the life. No one comes to the Father except through me. *John 14:1–6*

25. The last supper

When the hour for Passover came, Jesus took his place at the table, and the apostles with him. He said to them, "I have eagerly desired to eat this Passover with you before I suffer; Then he took a loaf of bread, and when he had given thanks, he broke it and gave it to them, saying, "This is my body, which is given for you. Do this in remembrance of me." And he did the same with the cup after supper, saying, "This cup that is poured out for you is the new covenant in my blood." *Luke 22:14–15, 19–20*

26. Jesus dies on the cross

The soldiers brought Jesus to the place called Golgotha (which means the place of a skull). And they offered him wine mixed with myrrh; but he did not take it. And they crucified him, and divided his clothes among them, casting lots to decide what each should take. It was nine o'clock in the morning when they crucified him. The inscription of the charge against him read, "The King of the Jews." And with him they crucified two bandits, one on his right and one on his left. Those who passed by derided him, shaking their heads and saying, "Aha! You who would destroy the temple and build it in three days, save yourself, and come down from the cross!" In the same way the chief priests, along with the scribes, were also mocking him among themselves and saying, "He saved others; he cannot save himself. Let the Messiah, the King of Israel, come down from the cross now, so that we may see and believe." Those who were crucified with him also taunted him.

When it was noon, darkness came over the whole land until three in the afternoon. At three o'clock Jesus cried out with a loud voice, "Eloi, Eloi, lema sabachthani?" which means, "My God, my God, why have you forsaken me?" When some of the bystanders heard it, they said, "Listen, he is calling for Elijah." And someone ran, filled a sponge with sour wine, put it on a stick, and gave it to him to drink, saying, "Wait, let us see whether Elijah will come to take him down." Then Jesus gave a loud cry and breathed his last. And the curtain of the temple was torn in two, from top to bottom. Now when the centurion, who stood facing him, saw that in this way he breathed his last, he said, "Truly this man was God's Son!"

Mark 15:22–39

27. The empty tomb

When the sabbath was over, Mary Magdalene, and Mary the mother of James, and Salome bought spices, so that they might go and anoint him. And very early on the first day of the week, when the sun had risen, they went to the tomb. They had been saying to one another, "Who will roll away the stone for us from the entrance to the tomb?" When they looked up, they saw that the stone, which was very large, had already been rolled back. As they entered the tomb, they saw a young man, dressed in a white robe, sitting on the right side; and they were alarmed. But he said to them, "Do not be alarmed; you are looking for Jesus of Nazareth, who was crucified. He has been raised; he is not here. Look, there is the place they laid him. But go, tell his disciples and Peter that he is going ahead of you to Galilee; there you will see him, just as he told you." So they went out and fled from the tomb, for terror and amazement had seized them; and they said nothing to anyone, for they were afraid.

Mark 16:1–8

28. The risen Christ appears

When it was evening on that day, the first day of the week, and the doors of the house where the disciples had met were locked for fear of the Jews, Jesus came and stood among them and said, "Peace be with you." After he said this, he showed them his hands and his side. Then the disciples rejoiced when they saw the Lord. Jesus said to them again, "Peace be with you. As the Father has sent me, so I send you." When he had said this, he breathed on them and said to them, "Receive the Holy Spirit. If you forgive the sins of any, they are forgiven them; if you retain the sins of any, they are retained."

John 20:19–23

29. The great commission

Jesus came to his disciples and said to them, "All authority in heaven and on earth has been given to me. Go therefore and make disciples of all nations, baptizing them in the name of the Father and of the Son and of the Holy Spirit, and teaching them to obey everything that I have commanded you. And remember, I am with you always, to the end of the age."   *Matthew 28:18–20*

30. Jesus ascends into heaven

When the disciples had come together with Jesus, he said, "You will receive power when the Holy Spirit has come upon you; and you will be my witnesses in Jerusalem, in all Judea and Samaria, and to the ends of the earth." When he had said this, as they were watching, he was lifted up, and a cloud took him out of their sight. While he was going and they were gazing up toward heaven, suddenly two men in white robes stood by them. They said, "Men of Galilee, why do you stand looking up toward heaven? This Jesus, who has been taken up from you into heaven, will come in the same way as you saw him go into heaven."   *Acts 1:8–11*

31. The Holy Spirit comes to the Church

When the day of Pentecost had come, they were all together in one place. And suddenly from heaven there came a sound like the rush of a violent wind, and it filled the entire house where they were sitting. Divided tongues, as of fire, appeared among them, and a tongue rested on each of them. All of them were filled with the Holy Spirit and began to speak in other languages, as the Spirit gave them ability.

Now there were devout Jews from every nation under heaven living in Jerusalem. And at this sound the crowd gathered and was bewildered, because each one heard them speaking in the native language of each.

But Peter, standing with the eleven, raised his voice and addressed them, "Men of Judea and all who live in Jerusalem, let this be known to you, and listen to what I say. You that are Israelites, listen to what I have to say: Jesus of Nazareth, a man attested to you by

God with deeds of power, wonders, and signs that God did through him among you, as you yourselves know — this man, handed over to you according to the definite plan and foreknowledge of God, you crucified and killed by the hands of those outside the law. But God raised him up, having freed him from death, because it was impossible for him to be held in its power. Being therefore exalted at the right hand of God, and having received from the Father the promise of the Holy Spirit, he has poured out this that you both see and hear."

Now when they heard this, they were cut to the heart and said to Peter and to the other apostles, "Brothers, what should we do?" Peter said to them, "Repent, and be baptized every one of you in the name of Jesus Christ so that your sins may be forgiven; and you will receive the gift of the Holy Spirit. For the promise is for you, for your children, and for all who are far away, everyone whom the Lord our God calls to him." So those who welcomed his message were baptized, and that day about three thousand persons were added. They devoted themselves to the apostles' teaching and fellowship, to the breaking of bread and the prayers   *Acts 2:1–6, 14a, 22–24, 33, 37–39, 41–42*

32. Marks of the true Christian

Let love be genuine; hate what is evil, hold fast to what is good; love one another with mutual affection; outdo one another in showing honor. Do not lag in zeal, be ardent in spirit, serve the Lord. Rejoice in hope, be patient in suffering, persevere in prayer. Contribute to the needs of the saints; extend hospitality to strangers. Bless those who persecute you; bless and do not curse them. Rejoice with those who rejoice, weep with those who weep. Live in harmony with one another; do not be haughty, but associate with the lowly; do not claim to be wiser than you are. Do not repay anyone evil for evil, but take thought for what is noble in the sight of all. If it is possible, so far as it depends on you, live peaceably with all. Beloved, never avenge yourselves, but leave room for the wrath of God; for it is written, "Vengeance is mine, I will repay, says the Lord." No, "if your enemies are hungry, feed them; if they are thirsty, give them something to drink; for by doing this you will heap burning coals on their heads." Do not be overcome by evil, but overcome evil with good.   *Romans 12:9–21*

33. Christians are members of Christ's body

The cup of blessing that we bless, is it not a sharing in the blood of Christ? The bread that we break, is it not a sharing in the body of Christ? Because there is one bread, we who are many are one body, for we all partake of the one bread.   *1 Corinthians 10:16–17*

34. Paul explains the gifts of the Spirit

There are varieties of gifts, but the same Spirit; and there are varieties of services, but the same Lord; and there are varieties of activities, but it is the same God who activates all of them in everyone. To each is given the manifestation of the Spirit for the common good. To one is given through the Spirit the utterance of wisdom, and to another the utterance of knowledge according to the same Spirit, to another faith by the same Spirit, to another gifts of healing by the one Spirit, to another the working of miracles, to another prophecy, to another the discernment of spirits, to another various kinds of tongues, to another the interpretation of tongues. All these are activated by one and the same Spirit, who allots to each one individually just as the Spirit chooses.

For just as the body is one and has many members, and all the members of the body, though many, are one body, so it is with Christ. For in the one Spirit we were all baptized into one body — Jews or Greeks, slaves or free — and we were all made to drink of one Spirit.   *1 Corinthians 12:4–13*

35. Christian love

Love is patient; love is kind; love is not envious or boastful or arrogant or rude. It does not insist on its own way; it is not irritable or resentful; it does not rejoice in wrongdoing, but rejoices in the truth. It bears all things, believes all things, hopes all things, endures all things. Love never ends.   *1 Corinthians 13:4–8a*

36. Christian conduct

As God's chosen ones, holy and beloved, clothe yourselves with compassion, kindness, humility, meekness, and patience. Bear with one another and, if anyone has a complaint against another, forgive each other; just as the Lord has forgiven you, so you also must forgive. Above all, clothe yourselves with love, which binds everything together in perfect harmony. And let the peace of Christ rule in your hearts, to which indeed you were called in the one body. And be thankful. *Colossians 3:12–15*

37. Do not worry

Rejoice in the Lord always; again I will say, Rejoice. Let your gentleness be known to everyone. The Lord is near. Do not worry about anything, but in everything by prayer and supplication with thanksgiving let your requests be made known to God. And the peace of God, which surpasses all understanding, will guard your hearts and your minds in Christ Jesus. Finally, beloved, whatever is true, whatever is honorable, whatever is just, whatever is pure, whatever is pleasing, whatever is commendable, if there is any excellence and if there is anything worthy of praise, think about these things. Keep on doing the things that you have learned and received and heard and seen in me, and the God of peace will be with you. *Philippians 4:4–9*

38. Our merciful High Priest

Since we have a great high priest who has passed through the heavens, Jesus, the Son of God, let us hold fast to our confession. For we do not have a high priest who is unable to sympathize with our weaknesses, but we have one who in every respect has been tested as we are, yet without sin. Let us therefore approach the throne of grace with boldness, so that we may receive mercy and find grace to help in time of need. *Hebrews 4:14–16*

39. The Church's ministry to the sick

Are any among you suffering? They should pray. Are any cheerful? They should sing songs of praise. Are any among you sick? They should call for the elders of the church and have them pray over them, anointing them with oil in the name of the Lord. The prayer of faith will save the sick, and the Lord will raise them up; and anyone who has committed sins will be forgiven. Therefore confess your sins to one another, and pray for one another, so that you may be healed. The prayer of the righteous is powerful and effective.

James 5:13–16a

40. *"Who will separate us?"*

Who will separate us from the love of Christ? Will hardship, or distress, or persecution, or famine, or nakedness, or peril, or sword? No, in all these things we are more than conquerors through him who loved us. For I am convinced that neither death, nor life, nor angels, nor rulers, nor things present, nor things to come, nor powers, nor height, nor depth, nor anything else in all creation, will be able to separate us from the love of God in Christ Jesus our Lord.

Romans 8:35, 37–39

41. *The resurrection of the dead*

Listen, I will tell you a mystery! We will not all die, but we will all be changed, in a moment, in the twinkling of an eye, at the last trumpet. For the trumpet will sound, and the dead will be raised imperishable, and we will be changed. For this perishable body must put on imperishability, and this mortal body must put on immortality. When this perishable body puts on imperishability, and this mortal body puts on immortality, then the saying that is written will be fulfilled: "Death has been swallowed up in victory." "Where, O death, is your victory? Where, O death, is your sting?" The sting of death is sin, and the power of sin is the law. But thanks be to God, who gives us the victory through our Lord Jesus Christ.   *1 Corinthians 15:51–57*

42. *Christ will come again*

John to the seven churches that are in Asia: Grace to you and peace from him who is and who was and who is to come, and from the seven spirits who are before his throne, and from Jesus Christ, the faithful witness, the firstborn of the dead, and the ruler of the kings of the earth.

To him who loves us and freed us from our sins by his blood, and made us to be a kingdom, priests serving his God and Father, to him be glory and dominion forever and ever. Amen. Look! He is coming with the clouds; every eye will see him, even those who pierced him; and on his account all the tribes of the earth will wail. So it is to be. Amen.

"I am the Alpha and the Omega," says the Lord God, who is and who was and who is to come, the Almighty.   *Revelation 1:4–8*

43. *"I am making all things new."*

I saw a new heaven and a new earth; for the first heaven and the first earth had passed away, and the sea was no more. And I saw the holy city, the new Jerusalem, coming down out of heaven from God, prepared as a bride adorned for her husband. And I heard a loud voice from the throne saying, "See, the home of God is among mortals. He will dwell with them as their God; they will be his peoples, and God himself will be with them; he will wipe every tear from their eyes. Death will be no more; mourning and crying and pain will be no more, for the first things have passed away." And the one who was seated on the throne said, "See, I am making all things new."   *Revelation 21:1–5a*

Psalms

PSALMS

The Psalms are the prayers and hymns of the Hebrew people, and the part of the Bible especially intended for use in public or private worship. They are given here in the translation used in the Book of Common Prayer of the Episcopal Church. Other Churches use different translations of the Psalms, but the meaning is the same.

Because they were used by Jesus himself, Christians interpret many of the Psalms in a special way. For example, because Christ spoke the opening words of Psalm 22 while dying on the cross, Christians understand the whole Psalm as a prayer of Jesus. Similarly, Christians interpret many of the references to "Israel," "Zion," and "Jerusalem" as applying also to the Christian Church.

When Psalms are used in private meditation, it is helpful to stop after each Psalm and offer a brief prayer — in one's own words — about something the Psalm has brought to mind.

A table of suggested Psalms for morning and evening is on page 17.

The asterisks (*) at the ends of lines show where the chant changes when the Psalms are sung. When they are read, a pause may be made at each asterisk.

The following doxology (statement of praise) may be said after the Psalms appointed for morning and evening

Glory to the Father, and to the Son,
    and to the Holy Spirit: *
as it was in the beginning, is now,
    and will be for ever. Amen.

For Psalms in Spanish, see pages 105–109.

A GUIDE TO THE PSALMS

FOR THE CHURCH YEAR

Advent 24, 63, 67, 85, 146
Christmas 85, 98, 150
Epiphany 67, 100, 146
Sunday after Epiphany 23, 46, 63, 84, 95, 121, 122
Lent 1, 22, 51, 103, 130
Easter Season 114, 118, 146, 150
Ascension Day 24, 98, 150
The Day of Pentecost 46, 122, 139
Trinity Sunday 100, 146, 150
Other Sundays after Pentecost *Any Psalm may be chosen*
Saint's Days and Feasts 46, 63, 67, 95, 98, 103, 146, 150
Thanksgiving Day 65, 67, 100
Other National Days 67, 98, 100, 146

FOR PARTICULAR NEEDS

God the Creator 65, 95, 100, 146
God the Redeemer 103, 114, 118, 130
God the Holy Spirit 51, 139
Baptism or Confirmation 23, 84, 122, 139
Burial and Memorial Services 23, 46, 121, 130, 139
The Church 46, 84, 122
God's Law 1, 146
God's Protection 23, 46, 91, 121, 139
In Harm's Way 23, 91
Holy Communion 23, 63, 84, 122
Meditations 103, 139
Praise 67, 95, 98, 100, 103, 146, 150
Prayer for Help 121, 130
Prayer for Reassurance 23, 46, 139
Repentance 51, 130
Sickness 23, 51, 121, 130, 139
Thanksgiving for Deliverance 103, 146

Psalm 1. *The two ways*

Happy are they who have not walked in the counsel of the wicked, *
  nor lingered in the way of sinners,
  nor sat in the seats of the scornful!
Their delight is in the law of the LORD, *
  and they meditate on his law day and night.
They are like trees planted by streams of water,
bearing fruit in due season, with leaves that do not wither; *
  everything they do shall prosper.
It is not so with the wicked; *
  they are like chaff which the wind blows away.
Therefore the wicked shall not stand upright when judgment
    comes, *
  nor the sinner in the council of the righteous.
For the LORD knows the way of the righteous, *
  but the way of the wicked is doomed.

Psalm 22:1–11, 14–18. *Jesus' prayer from the cross*

My God, my God, why have you forsaken me? *
  and are so far from my cry
  and from the words of my distress?
O my God, I cry in the daytime, but you do not answer; *
  by night as well, but I find no rest.
Yet you are the Holy One, *
  enthroned upon the praises of Israel.
Our forefathers put their trust in you; *
  they trusted, and you delivered them.
They cried out to you and were delivered; *
  they trusted in you and were not put to shame.
But as for me, I am a worm and no man, *
  scorned by all and despised by the people.
All who see me laugh me to scorn; *
  they curl their lips and wag their heads, saying,
"He trusted in the LORD; let him deliver him; *
  let him rescue him, if he delights in him."
Yet you are he who took me out of the womb, *
  and kept me safe upon my mother's breast.

I have been entrusted to you ever since I was born; *
    you were my God when I was still in my mother's womb.
Be not far from me, for trouble is near, *
    and there is none to help.
I am poured out like water;
all my bones are out of joint; *
    my heart within my breast is melting wax.
My mouth is dried out like a pot-sherd;
my tongue sticks to the roof of my mouth; *
    and you have laid me in the dust of the grave.
Packs of dogs close me in,
and gangs of evildoers circle around me; *
    they pierce my hands and my feet;
    I can count all my bones.
They stare and gloat over me; *
    they divide my garments among them;
    they cast lots for my clothing.
Be not far away, O LORD; *
    you are my strength; hasten to help me.

Psalm 23. *The good shepherd*

The LORD is my shepherd; *
    I shall not be in want.
He makes me lie down in green pastures *
    and leads me beside still waters.
He revives my soul *
    and guides me along right pathways for his Name's sake.
Though I walk through the valley of the shadow of death,
I shall fear no evil, *
    for you are with me;
    your rod and your staff, they comfort me.
You spread a table before me in the presence of those who
        trouble me; *
    you have anointed my head with oil,
    and my cup is running over.

Surely your goodness and mercy shall follow me all the days of
 my life, *
  and I will dwell in the house of the LORD for ever.

Psalm 23. *King James Version*

The LORD is my shepherd; *
  I shall not want.
He maketh me to lie down in green pastures; *
  he leadeth me beside the still waters.
He restoreth my soul; *
  he leadeth me in the paths of righteousness
  for his Name's sake.
Yea, though I walk through the valley of the shadow of death,
I will fear no evil; *
  for thou art with me;
  thy rod and thy staff, they comfort me.
Thou preparest a table before me
in the presence of mine enemies; *
  thou anointest my head with oil;
  my cup runneth over.
Surely goodness and mercy shall follow me
all the days of my life, *
  and I will dwell in the house of the LORD for ever.

Psalm 24. *The Lord enters his holy place*

The earth is the LORD's and all that is in it, *
  the world and all who dwell therein.
For it is he who founded it upon the seas *
  and made it firm upon the rivers of the deep.
"Who can ascend the hill of the LORD? *
  and who can stand in his holy place?"
"Those who have clean hands and a pure heart, *
  who have not pledged themselves to falsehood,
  nor sworn by what is a fraud.
They shall receive a blessing from the LORD *
  and a just reward from the God of their salvation."

Such is the generation of those who seek him, *
    of those who seek your face, O God of Jacob.
Lift up your heads, O gates;
lift them high, O everlasting doors; *
    and the King of glory shall come in.
"Who is this King of glory?" *
    "The LORD, strong and mighty,
    the LORD, mighty in battle."
Lift up your heads, O gates;
lift them high, O everlasting doors; *
    and the King of glory shall come in.
"Who is he, this King of glory?" *
    "The LORD of hosts,
    he is the King of glory."

Psalm 46. *God, the source of peace*

God is our refuge and strength, *
    a very present help in trouble.
Therefore we will not fear, though the earth be moved, *
    and though the mountains be toppled into the depths of the sea;
Though its waters rage and foam, *
    and though the mountains tremble at its tumult.
The LORD of hosts is with us; *
    the God of Jacob is our stronghold.
There is a river whose streams make glad the city of God, *
    the holy habitation of the Most High.
God is in the midst of her;
she shall not be overthrown; *
    God shall help her at the break of day.
The nations make much ado, and the kingdoms are shaken; *
    God has spoken, and the earth shall melt away.
The LORD of hosts is with us; *
    the God of Jacob is our stronghold.
Come now and look upon the works of the LORD, *
    what awesome things he has done on earth.

It is he who makes war to cease in all the world; *
    he breaks the bow, and shatters the spear,
    and burns the shields with fire.
"Be still, then, and know that I am God; *
    I will be exalted among the nations;
    I will be exalted in the earth."
The LORD of hosts is with us; *
    the God of Jacob is our stronghold.

Psalm 51:1–18. *Prayer for mercy and for God's Spirit*

Have mercy on me, O God, according to your loving-kindness; *
    in your great compassion blot out my offenses.
Wash me through and through from my wickedness *
    and cleanse me from my sin.
For I know my transgressions, *
    and my sin is ever before me.
Against you only have I sinned *
    and done what is evil in your sight.
And so you are justified when you speak *
    and upright in your judgment.
Indeed, I have been wicked from my birth, *
    a sinner from my mother's womb.
For behold, you look for truth deep within me, *
    and will make me understand wisdom secretly.
Purge me from my sin, and I shall be pure; *
    wash me, and I shall be clean indeed.
Make me hear of joy and gladness, *
    that the body you have broken may rejoice.
Hide your face from my sins *
    and blot out all my iniquities.
Create in me a clean heart, O God, *
    and renew a right spirit within me.
Cast me not away from your presence *
    and take not your holy Spirit from me.
Give me the joy of your saving help again *
    and sustain me with your bountiful Spirit.

I shall teach your ways to the wicked, *
    and sinners shall return to you.
Deliver me from death, O God, *
    and my tongue shall sing of your righteousness,
      O God of my salvation.
Open my lips, O Lord, *
    and my mouth shall proclaim your praise.
Had you desired it, I would have offered sacrifice, *
    but you take no delight in burnt-offerings.
The sacrifice of God is a troubled spirit; *
    a broken and contrite heart, O God, you will not despise.

Psalm 63:1–8. Hunger and thirst for God

O God, you are my God; eagerly I seek you; *
    my soul thirsts for you, my flesh faints for you,
      as in a barren and dry land where there is no water.
Therefore I have gazed upon you in your holy place, *
    that I might behold your power and your glory.
For your loving-kindness is better than life itself; *
    my lips shall give you praise.
So will I bless you as long as I live *
    and lift up my hands in your Name.
My soul is content, as with marrow and fatness, *
    and my mouth praises you with joyful lips,
When I remember you upon my bed, *
    and meditate on you in the night watches.
For you have been my helper, *
    and under the shadow of your wings I will rejoice.
My soul clings to you; *
    your right hand holds me fast.

Psalm 65. Thanksgiving for God's blessings

You are to be praised, O God, in Zion; *
    to you shall vows be performed in Jerusalem.
To you that hear prayer shall all flesh come, *
    because of their transgressions.

Our sins are stronger than we are, *
    but you will blot them out.
Happy are they whom you choose
and draw to your courts to dwell there! *
    they will be satisfied by the beauty of your house,
    by the holiness of your temple.
Awesome things will you show us in your righteousness,
O God of our salvation, *
    O Hope of all the ends of the earth
    and of the seas that are far away.
You make fast the mountains by your power; *
    they are girded about with might.
You still the roaring of the seas, *
    the roaring of their waves,
    and the clamor of the peoples.
Those who dwell at the ends of the earth will tremble at your
        marvelous signs; *
    you make the dawn and the dusk to sing for joy.
You visit the earth and water it abundantly;
you make it very plenteous; *
    the river of God is full of water.
You prepare the grain, *
    for so you provide for the earth.
You drench the furrows and smooth out the ridges; *
    with heavy rain you soften the ground and bless its increase.
You crown the year with your goodness, *
    and your paths overflow with plenty.
May the fields of the wilderness be rich for grazing, *
    and the hills be clothed with joy.
May the meadows cover themselves with flocks,
    and the valleys cloak themselves with grain; *
    let them shout for joy and sing.

Psalm 67. Song of blessing

May God be merciful to us and bless us, *
    show us the light of his countenance and come to us.

Let your ways be known upon earth, *
    your saving health among all nations.
Let the peoples praise you, O God; *
    let all the peoples praise you.
Let the nations be glad and sing for joy, *
    for you judge the peoples with equity
    and guide all the nations upon earth.
Let the peoples praise you, O God; *
    let all the peoples praise you.
The earth has brought forth her increase; *
    may God, our own God, give us his blessing.
May God give us his blessing, *
    and may all the ends of the earth stand in awe of him.

Psalm 84. Longing for God's dwelling

How dear to me is your dwelling, O LORD of hosts! *
    My soul has a desire and longing for the courts of the LORD;
    my heart and my flesh rejoice in the living God.
The sparrow has found her a house
and the swallow a nest where she may lay her young; *
    by the side of your altars, O LORD of hosts,
    my King and my God.
Happy are they who dwell in your house! *
    they will always be praising you.
Happy are the people whose strength is in you! *
    whose hearts are set on the pilgrims' way.
Those who go through the desolate valley will find it a place
        of springs, *
    for the early rains have covered it with pools of water.
They will climb from height to height, *
    and the God of gods will reveal himself in Zion.
LORD God of hosts, hear my prayer; *
    hearken, O God of Jacob.
Behold our defender, O God; *
    and look upon the face of your Anointed.

For one day in your courts is better than a thousand in my
    own room, *
    and to stand at the threshold of the house of my God
    than to dwell in the tents of the wicked.
For the LORD God is both sun and shield; *
    he will give grace and glory;
No good thing will the LORD withhold *
    from those who walk with integrity.
O LORD of hosts, *
    happy are they who put their trust in you!

Psalm 85:8–13. *God's word of peace*

I will listen to what the LORD God is saying, *
    for he is speaking peace to his faithful people
    and to those who turn their hearts to him.
Truly, his salvation is very near to those who fear him, *
    that his glory may dwell in our land.
Mercy and truth have met together; *
    righteousness and peace have kissed each other.
Truth shall spring up from the earth, *
    and righteousness shall look down from heaven.
The LORD will indeed grant prosperity, *
    and our land will yield its increase.
Righteousness shall go before him, *
    and peace shall be a pathway for his feet.

Psalm 91. *God our protector*

He who dwells in the shelter of the Most High, *
    abides under the shadow of the Almighty.
He shall say to the LORD,
    "You are my refuge and my stronghold, *
    my God in whom I put my trust."
He shall deliver you from the snare of the hunter *
    and from the deadly pestilence.
He shall cover you with his pinions,
and you shall find refuge under his wings; *
    his faithfulness shall be a shield and buckler.

You shall not be afraid of any terror by night, *
   nor of the arrow that flies by day;
Of the plague that stalks in the darkness, *
   nor of the sickness that lays waste at mid-day.
A thousand shall fall at your side
and ten thousand at your right hand, *
   but it shall not come near you.
Your eyes have only to behold *
   to see the reward of the wicked.
Because you have made the LORD your refuge, *
   and the Most High your habitation,
There shall no evil happen to you, *
   neither shall any plague come near your dwelling.
For he shall give his angels charge over you, *
   to keep you in all your ways.
They shall bear you in their hands, *
   lest you dash your foot against a stone.
You shall tread upon the lion and adder; *
   you shall trample the young lion and the serpent under your feet.
Because he is bound to me in love,
therefore will I deliver him; *
   I will protect him, because he knows my Name.
He shall call upon me, and I will answer him; *
   I am with him in trouble;
   I will rescue him and bring him to honor.
With long life will I satisfy him, *
   and show him my salvation.

Psalm 95:1–7. *A call to worship*

Come, let us sing to the LORD; *
   let us shout for joy to the Rock of our salvation.
Let us come before his presence with thanksgiving *
   and raise a loud shout to him with psalms.
For the LORD is a great God, *
   and a great King above all gods.
In his hand are the caverns of the earth, *
   and the heights of the hills are his also.

The sea is his, for he made it,*
  and his hands have molded the dry land.
Come, let us bow down, and bend the knee,*
  and kneel before the LORD our Maker.
For he is our God,
and we are the people of his pasture and the sheep of his hand.*
  Oh, that today you would hearken to his voice!

Psalm 98. *God, victor and judge*

Sing to the LORD a new song,*
  for he has done marvelous things.
With his right hand and his holy arm*
  has he won for himself the victory.
The LORD has made known his victory;*
  his righteousness has he openly shown in the sight of the nations.
He remembers his mercy and faithfulness to the house of Israel,*
  and all the ends of the earth have seen the victory of our God.
Shout with joy to the LORD, all you lands;*
  lift up your voice, rejoice, and sing.
Sing to the LORD with the harp,*
  with the harp and the voice of song.
With trumpets and the sound of the horn*
  shout with joy before the King, the LORD.
Let the sea make a noise and all that is in it,*
  the lands and those who dwell therein.
Let the rivers clap their hands,*
  and let the hills ring out with joy before the LORD,
  when he comes to judge the earth.
In righteousness shall he judge the world*
  and the peoples with equity.

Psalm 100. *God, creator and shepherd*

Be joyful in the LORD, all you lands;*
  serve the LORD with gladness
  and come before his presence with a song.

Know this: The LORD himself is God; *
  he himself has made us, and we are his;
  we are his people and the sheep of his pasture.
Enter his gates with thanksgiving;
  go into his courts with praise; *
  give thanks to him and call upon his Name.
For the LORD is good;
his mercy is everlasting; *
  and his faithfulness endures from age to age.

Psalm 103. *Praise for God's mercy*

Bless the LORD, O my soul, *
  and all that is within me, bless his holy Name.
Bless the LORD, O my soul, *
  and forget not all his benefits.
He forgives all your sins *
  and heals all your infirmities;
He redeems your life from the grave *
  and crowns you with mercy and loving-kindness;
He satisfies you with good things, *
  and your youth is renewed like an eagle's.
The LORD executes righteousness *
  and judgment for all who are oppressed.
He made his ways known to Moses *
  and his works to the children of Israel.
The LORD is full of compassion and mercy, *
  slow to anger and of great kindness.
He will not always accuse us, *
  nor will he keep his anger for ever.
He has not dealt with us according to our sins, *
  nor rewarded us according to our wickedness.
For as the heavens are high above the earth, *
  so is his mercy great upon those who fear him.
As far as the east is from the west, *
  so far has he removed our sins from us.
As a father cares for his children, *
  so does the LORD care for those who fear him.

For he himself knows whereof we are made; *
  he remembers that we are but dust.
Our days are like the grass; *
  we flourish like a flower of the field;
When the wind goes over it, it is gone, *
  and its place shall know it no more.
But the merciful goodness of the LORD endures for ever on those
      who fear him, *
  and his righteousness on children's children;
On those who keep his covenant *
  and remember his commandments and do them.
The LORD has set his throne in heaven, *
  and his kingship has dominion over all.
Bless the LORD, you angels of his,
you mighty ones who do his bidding, *
  and hearken to the voice of his word.
Bless the LORD, all you his hosts, *
  you ministers of his who do his will.
Bless the LORD, all you works of his,
  in all places of his dominion; *
bless the LORD, O my soul.

Psalm 114. *The wonders of the Exodus*

Hallelujah!
When Israel came out of Egypt, *
  the house of Jacob from a people of strange speech,
Judah became God's sanctuary *
  and Israel his dominion.
The sea beheld it and fled; *
  Jordan turned and went back.
The mountains skipped like rams, *
  and the little hills like young sheep.
What ailed you, O sea, that you fled? *
  O Jordan, that you turned back?
You mountains, that you skipped like rams? *
  you little hills like young sheep?

Tremble, O earth, at the presence of the Lord, *
  at the presence of the God of Jacob,
Who turned the hard rock into a pool of water *
  and flint-stone into a flowing spring.

Psalm 118:1–6, 19–24.   *Thanksgiving for salvation*

Give thanks to the Lord, for he is good; *
  his mercy endures for ever.
Let Israel now proclaim, *
"His mercy endures for ever."
Let the house of Aaron now proclaim, *
"His mercy endures for ever."
Let those who fear the Lord now proclaim, *
"His mercy endures for ever."
I called to the Lord in my distress; *
  the Lord answered by setting me free.
The Lord is at my side, therefore I will not fear; *
  what can anyone do to me?
Open for me the gates of righteousness; *
  I will enter them;
  I will offer thanks to the Lord.
"This is the gate of the Lord; *
  he who is righteous may enter."
I will give thanks to you, for you answered me *
  and have become my salvation.
The same stone which the builders rejected *
  has become the chief cornerstone.
This is the Lord's doing, *
  and it is marvelous in our eyes.
On this day the Lord has acted; *
  we will rejoice and be glad in it.

Psalm 121.   *God our guardian*

I lift up my eyes to the hills; *
  from where is my help to come?
My help comes from the Lord, *
  the maker of heaven and earth.

He will not let your foot be moved *
  and he who watches over you will not fall asleep.
Behold, he who keeps watch over Israel *
  shall neither slumber nor sleep;
The LORD himself watches over you; *
  the LORD is your shade at your right hand,
So that the sun shall not strike you by day, *
  nor the moon by night.
The LORD shall preserve you from all evil; *
  it is he who shall keep you safe.
The LORD shall watch over your going out and your coming in, *
  from this time forth for evermore.

Psalm 122. *Jerusalem, a symbol of the Church*

I was glad when they said to me, *
  "Let us go to the house of the LORD."
Now our feet are standing *
  within your gates, O Jerusalem.
Jerusalem is built as a city *
  that is at unity with itself;
To which the tribes go up,
the tribes of the LORD, *
  the assembly of Israel,
  to praise the Name of the LORD.
For there are the thrones of judgment, *
  the thrones of the house of David.
Pray for the peace of Jerusalem: *
  "May they prosper who love you.
Peace be within your walls *
  and quietness within your towers.
For my brethren and companions' sake, *
  I pray for your prosperity.
Because of the house of the LORD our God, *
  I will seek to do you good."

Psalm 130. A cry from the depths

Out of the depths have I called to you, O LORD;
LORD, hear my voice; *
    let your ears consider well the voice of my supplication.
If you, LORD, were to note what is done amiss, *
    O LORD, who could stand?
For there is forgiveness with you; *
    therefore you shall be feared.
I wait for the LORD; my soul waits for him; *
    in his word is my hope.
My soul waits for the LORD,
more than watchmen for the morning, *
    more than watchmen for the morning.
O Israel, wait for the LORD, *
    for with the LORD there is mercy;
With him there is plenteous redemption, *
    and he shall redeem Israel from all their sins.

Psalm 139:1–11, 22–23. The all-knowing and ever-present God

LORD, you have searched me out and known me; *
    you know my sitting down and my rising up;
    you discern my thoughts from afar.
You trace my journeys and my resting-places *
    and are acquainted with all my ways.
Indeed, there is not a word on my lips, *
    but you, O LORD, know it altogether.
You press upon me behind and before *
    and lay your hand upon me.
Such knowledge is too wonderful for me; *
    it is so high that I cannot attain to it.
Where can I go then from your Spirit? *
    where can I flee from your presence?
If I climb up to heaven, you are there; *
    if I make the grave my bed, you are there also.
If I take the wings of the morning *
    and dwell in the uttermost parts of the sea,

Even there your hand will lead me *
  and your right hand hold me fast.
If I say, "Surely the darkness will cover me, *
  and the light around me turn to night,"
Darkness is not dark to you;
the night is as bright as the day; *
  darkness and light to you are both alike.
Search me out, O God, and know my heart; *
  try me and know my restless thoughts.
Look well whether there be any wickedness in me *
  and lead me in the way that is everlasting.

Psalm 146. *Hymn to God our helper*

Hallelujah!
Praise the LORD, O my soul! *
  I will praise the LORD as long as I live;
  I will sing praises to my God while I have my being.
Put not your trust in rulers, nor in any child of earth, *
  for there is no help in them.
When they breathe their last, they return to earth, *
  and in that day their thoughts perish.
Happy are they who have the God of Jacob for their help! *
  whose hope is in the LORD their God;
Who made heaven and earth, the seas, and all that is in them; *
  who keeps his promise for ever;
Who gives justice to those who are oppressed, *
  and food to those who hunger.
The LORD sets the prisoners free;
the LORD opens the eyes of the blind; *
  the LORD lifts up those who are bowed down;
The LORD loves the righteous;
the LORD cares for the stranger; *
  he sustains the orphan and widow,
  but frustrates the way of the wicked.
The LORD shall reign for ever, *
  your God, O Zion, throughout all generations.
  Hallelujah!

Psalm 150. *Praise from all creatures*

Hallelujah!
Praise God in his holy temple; *
   praise him in the firmament of his power.
Praise him for his mighty acts; *
   praise him for his excellent greatness.
Praise him with the blast of the ram's-horn; *
   praise him with lyre and harp.
Praise him with timbrel and dance; *
   praise him with strings and pipe.
Praise him with resounding cymbals; *
   praise him with loud-clanging cymbals.
Let everything that has breath *
   praise the LORD.
   Hallelujah!

Salmos

Salmo 23. *El buen pastor*

El Señor es mi pastor; *
   nada me faltará.
En verdes pastos me hace yacer; *
   me conduce hacia aguas tranquilas.
Aviva mi alma *
   y me guía por sendas seguras por amor de su Nombre.
Aunque ande en valle de sombra de muerte,
no temeré mal alguno; *
   porque tú estás conmigo;
   tu vara y tu cayado me infunden aliento.
Aderezarás mesa delante de mí
en presencia de mis angustiadores; *
   unges mi cabeza con óleo;
   mi copa está rebosando.
Ciertamente el bien y la misericordia me seguirán
todos los días de mi vida, *
   y en la casa del Señor moraré por largos días.

Salmos 98. *Dios, victorioso y juez*

Canten al Señor cántico nuevo, *
   porque ha hecho maravillas.
Con su diestra, y con su santo brazo, *
   ha alcanzado la victoria.
El Señor ha dado a conocer su victoria; *
   a la vista de las naciones ha descubierto su justicia.
Se acuerda de su misericordia y su fidelidad
para con la casa de Israel; *
   los confines de la tierra
      han visto la victoria de nuestro Dios.
Aclamen con júbilo al Señor, pueblos todos; *
   levanten la voz, gócense y canten.
Canten al Señor con el arpa, *
   con el arpa y la voz de cántico.
Con trompetas y al son de clarines, *
   aclamen con júbilo ante el Rey, el Señor.
Ruja el mar y cuanto contiene, *
   el mundo y los que en él habitan.
Den palmadas los ríos, aclamen los montes al Señor, *
   cuando llegue para juzgar la tierra.
Juzgará al mundo con justicia, *
   y a los pueblos con equidad.

Salmo 118:1–6, 19–24. *Acción de gracias por la salvación*

Den gracias al Señor, porque él es bueno; *
   para siempre es su misericordia.
Diga ahora Israel: *
   "Para siempre es su misericordia."
Diga ahora la casa de Aarón: *
   "Para siempre es su misericordia."
Digan ahora los que veneran al Señor: *
   "Para siempre es su misericordia."
En mi angustia invoqué al Señor; *
   me respondió el Señor, poniéndome a salvo.
El Señor está a mi lado; por tanto, no temeré; *
   ¿quién podrá dañarme?

Abranme las puertas de justicia; *
  entraré por ellas, y daré gracias al Señor.
"Esta es la puerta del Señor; *
  por ella entrarán los justos."
Daré gracias porque me respondiste, *
  y me has sido de salvación.
La misma piedra que desecharon los edificadores, *
  ha venido a ser la cabeza del ángulo.
Esto es lo que ha hecho el Señor, *
  y es maravilloso a nuestros ojos.
Este es el día en que actuó el Señor; *
  regocijémonos y alegrémonos en él.

Salmo 130. *Un clamor de lo profundo*

De lo profundo, oh Señor, a ti clamo;
Señor, escucha mi voz; *
  estén atentos tus oídos a la voz de mi súplica.
Si tú, oh Señor, notares los delitos, *
  ¿quién, oh Señor, podrá mantenerse?
Mas en ti hay perdón, *
  por tanto serás venerado.
Aguardo al Señor; le aguarda mi alma; *
  en su palabra está mi esperanza.
Mi alma aguarda al Señor,
más que los centinelas a la aurora, *
  más que los centinelas a la aurora.
Oh Israel, aguarda al Señor, *
  porque en el Señor hay misericordia;
Con él hay abundante redención, *
  y el redimirá a Israel de todos sus pecados.

Salmo 139:1–11, 22–23. *El Dios sapiente y omnipresente*

Oh Señor, tú me has probado y conocido; *
  conoces mi sentarme y mi levantarme;
  percibes de lejos mis pensamientos.
Observas mis viajes y mis lugares de reposo, *
  y todos mis caminos te son conocidos.

Aún no está la palabra en mis labios, *
    y he aquí, oh Señor, tú la conoces.
Me rodeas delante y detrás, *
    y sobre mí pones tu mano.
Tal conocimiento es demasiado maravilloso para mí; *
    sublime es, y no lo puedo alcanzar.
¿A dónde huiré de tu Espíritu? *
    ¿A dónde huiré de tu presencia?
Si subiere a los cielos, allí estás tú; *
    si en el abismo hiciere mi lecho, allí estás también.
Si tomare las alas del alba, *
    y habitare en el extremo del mar,
Aun allí me guiará tu mano, *
    y me asirá tu diestra.
Si dijere: "Ciertamente las tinieblas me encubrirán, *
    y aun la luz se hará noche alrededor de mí,"
Las tinieblas no son oscuras para ti;
    la noche resplandece como el día; *
    lo mismo te son las tinieblas que la luz;
Escudríñame, oh Dios, y conoce mi corazón; *
    pruébame, y conoce mis inquietudes.
Ve si hay en mí camino de perversidad, *
    y guíame en el camino eterno.

Salmo 146. *Himno a Dios nuestra ayuda*

¡Aleluya!
Alaba, alma mía, al Señor; *
    alabaré al Señor mientras viva;
    cantaré alabanzas a mi Dios mientras exista.
No confíes en los príncipes, ni en ningún hijo de Adán, *
    porque no hay en ellos seguridad.
Al exhalar el espíritu, vuelven al polvo, *
    y en ese día perecen todos sus planes.
¡Dichosos aquéllos cuya ayuda es el Dios de Jacob, *
    cuya esperanza está en el Señor su Dios!

El cual hizo los cielos y la tierra,
el mar, y cuanto en ellos hay, *
    que guarda su promesa para siempre;
Que hace justicia a los oprimidos, *
    y da pan a los hambrientos.
El Señor liberta a los cautivos;
el Señor abre los ojos a los ciegos; *
    el Señor levanta a los caídos;
El Señor ama a los justos;
el Señor protege a los forasteros; *
    sostiene al huérfano y a la viuda,
    pero trastorna el camino de los malvados.
Reinará el Señor para siempre, *
    tu Dios, oh Sión, de generación en generación.
    ¡Aleluya!

Services and Sacraments

A SERVICE OF WORSHIP

This service may be led by a chaplain or lay reader. In the absence of such a person, any Christian may lead this service.

Whenever possible, the leader should appoint other persons to read the Scripture Readings which precede the Gospel and to lead the Prayers of the People.

When circumstances permit, hymns should be sung at the places indicated. When necessary, however, they may be omitted.

The Scripture Readings should ordinarily be those appointed in the Lectionary of the Book of Common Prayer (or in the similar lectionary in the *Book of Worship for United States Forces*). When necessary, however, Readings from this book may be used instead. For suggested Readings, see page 65. For Psalms, see page 87. For hymns, see page 167.

If a shorter form of service is desired, one of the first two Readings may be omitted. In that case, the Psalm follows the Reading chosen.

If all do not have books, a member of the congregation may be appointed to read the Psalm. When the service is led by a chaplain, a sermon may follow the Gospel and the service may end with a priestly blessing. A licensed lay reader may read an authorized sermon. A chaplain or lay reader may also, instead of using this form of service, use the Liturgy of the Word from the Holy Eucharist, concluding it as indicated on page 134.

ORDER OF THE SERVICE

1. Opening Hymn.

2. Opening Prayer. *The leader may use one of the Prayers on pages 21–29, or some other prayer.*

3. First Reading. *From the Old Testament. In Easter Season it is customary to read from the Acts of the Apostles instead.*

4. Psalm. *Said by all together.*

5. Second Reading. *From any New Testament book except the Gospels.*

6. Hymn.

7. Gospel. *All stand for this reading.*

8. Response to the Gospel. *The leader, or some other person, may comment briefly on the Gospel passage. Alternatively, all may meditate on the passage, sitting in silence.*

9. Creed. *Either the Apostles' Creed (inside the front cover) or the Nicene Creed (page 130) may be said, or the Creed may be omitted.*

10. Prayers of the People. *One of the forms on pages 131–134 may be used, or other prayers may be said.*

11. The Lord's Prayer. *Said by all together.*

12. Closing Hymn.

The leader ends the service with one of the blessings on page 60 or with the following.

The grace of our Lord Jesus Christ, and the love of God, and the fellowship of the Holy Spirit, be with us all evermore. *Amen.*

2 Corinthians 13:14

ABOUT HOLY BAPTISM

Holy Baptism is the sacrament by which we are born again by water and the Spirit. In this sacrament God adopts us as his children, unites us to Christ in his death and resurrection, makes us members of Christ's Body the Church, forgives our sins, and gives us new life in the Holy Spirit.

Ordinarily, Baptism is administered at a celebration of the Holy Eucharist, especially on Easter Day, or on some other Sunday or feast day.

The Episcopal Church, like most churches, recognizes all Baptisms reverently performed with water in the Name of the Father, and of the Son, and of the Holy Spirit.

Adults desiring to be baptized should speak to the chaplain as soon as possible, in order that they may receive instruction in the Christian faith. They should also prepare themselves by repentance and prayer to receive this holy Sacrament.

When the Bishop is present at Baptism, the Bishop performs the Laying on of Hands (and anointing) that follows the administration of the water. Adults who receive this Laying on of Hands by the Bishop do not need to be confirmed later.

The service of Holy Baptism is the usual time for the Bishop to administer Confirmation and to receive persons baptized in some other Church into the Episcopal Church. It is also the time when persons who have abandoned the practice of the Christian religion may reaffirm their baptismal vows and be welcomed back by the Bishop.

For the form for Emergency Baptism, see pages 124–126.

HOLY BAPTISM

A hymn, psalm, or anthem may be sung.

The people standing, the Celebrant says

	Blessed be God: Father, Son, and Holy Spirit.
People	And blessed be his kingdom, now and for ever. Amen.

In place of the above, from Easter Day through the Day of Pentecost

Celebrant	Alleluia. Christ is risen.
People	The Lord is risen indeed. Alleluia.

In Lent and on other penitential occasions

Celebrant	Bless the Lord who forgives all our sins.
People	His mercy endures for ever.

The Celebrant then continues

	There is one Body and one Spirit;
People	There is one hope in God's call to us;
Celebrant	One Lord, one Faith, one Baptism;
People	One God and Father of all.
Celebrant	The Lord be with you.
People	And also with you.
Celebrant	Let us pray.

The Prayer of the Day

People	Amen.

At the principal service on a Sunday or other feast, the Prayer and Lessons are properly those of the Day. On other occasions they are selected from "At Baptism." (See Book of Common Prayer, pages 312 and 928.)

The Lessons

The people sit. One or two Lessons, as appointed, are read, the Reader first saying

A reading (Lesson) from _____ .

A citation giving chapter and verse may be added.

After each reading, the Reader may say

     The Word of the Lord.

People   Thanks be to God.

or the Reader may say

     Here ends the Reading (Epistle).

Silence may follow.

A psalm, hymn, or anthem may follow each Reading.

Then, all standing, the Deacon or a Priest reads the Gospel, first saying

     The Holy Gospel of our Lord Jesus Christ

     according to _____ .

People   Glory to you, Lord Christ.

The Sermon

Or the Sermon may be preached after the Peace.

Presentation and Examination of the Candidates

The Celebrant says
The Candidate(s) for Holy Baptism will now be presented.

Adults and Older Children

The candidates who are able to answer for themselves are presented individually by their Sponsors, as follows

Sponsor   I present _____ to receive the Sacrament of
      Baptism.

The Celebrant asks each candidate when presented
Do you desire to be baptized?
Candidate   I do.

Infants and Younger Children

Then the candidates unable to answer for themselves are presented individually by their Parents and Godparents, as follows:

Parents and Godparents
I present _____ to receive the Sacrament of Baptism.

When all have been presented the Celebrant asks the parents and godparents

Will you be responsible for seeing that the child you present is brought up in the Christian faith and life?

Parents and Godparents
I will, with God's help.

Celebrant
Will you by your prayers and witness help this child to grow into the full stature of Christ?

Parents and Godparents
I will, with God's help.

Then the Celebrants asks the following questions of the candidates who can speak for themselves, and of the parents and godparents who speak on behalf of the infants and younger children

Question	Do you renounce Satan and all the spiritual forces of wickedness that rebel against God?
Answer	I renounce them.
Question	Do you renounce the evil powers of this world which corrupt and destroy the creatures of God?
Answer	I renounce them.
Question	Do you renounce all sinful desires that draw you from the love of God?
Answer	I renounce them.

Question	Do you turn to Jesus Christ and accept him as your Savior?
Answer	I do.
Question	Do you put your whole trust in his grace and love?
Answer	I do.
Question	Do you promise to follow and obey him as your Lord?
Answer	I do.

When there are others to be presented, the Bishop says
The other Candidate(s) will now be presented.

Presenters	I present *these persons* for Confirmation.
or	I present *these persons* to be received into this Communion.
or	I present *these persons* who *desire* to reaffirm *their* baptismal vows.

The Bishop asks the candidates
Do you reaffirm your renunciation of evil?

Candidate	I do.
Bishop	Do you renew your commitment to Jesus Christ?
Candidate	I do, and with God's grace I will follow him as my Savior and Lord.

After all have been presented, the Celebrant addresses the congregation, saying
Will you who witness these vows do all in your power to support *these persons* in *their* life in Christ?

People	We will.

The Celebrant then says these or similar words
Let us join with *those* who *are* committing *themselves* to Christ and renew our own baptismal covenant.

The Baptismal Covenant

Celebrant	Do you believe in God the Father?
People	I believe in God, the Father almighty, creator of heaven and earth.

Celebrant	Do you believe in Jesus Christ, the Son of God?
People	I believe in Jesus Christ, his only Son, our Lord.

He was conceived by the power of the Holy Spirit
and born of the Virgin Mary.
He suffered under Pontius Pilate,
was crucified, died, and was buried.
He descended to the dead.
On the third day he rose again.
He ascended into heaven,
and is seated at the right hand of the Father.
He will come again to judge the living and
the dead.

Celebrant	Do you believe in God the Holy Spirit?
People	I believe in the Holy Spirit, the holy catholic Church, the communion of saints, the forgiveness of sins, the resurrection of the body, and the life everlasting.
Celebrant	Will you continue in the apostles' teaching and fellowship, in the breaking of bread, and in the prayers?
People	I will, with God's help.
Celebrant	Will you persevere in resisting evil, and, whenever you fall into sin, repent and return to the Lord?
People	I will, with God's help.
Celebrant	Will you proclaim by word and example the Good News of God in Christ?
People	I will, with God's help.
Celebrant	Will you seek and serve Christ in all persons, loving your neighbor as yourself?
People	I will, with God's help.

Celebrant	Will you strive for justice and peace among all people, and respect the dignity of every human being?
People	I will, with God's help.

Prayers for the Candidates

The Celebrant then says to the congregation

Let us pray for *these persons* who *are* to receive the Sacrament of new birth [and for those (this person) who *have* renewed *their* commitment to Christ.]

A person appointed leads the following petitions

Leader	Deliver *them*, O Lord, from the way of sin and death.
People	Lord, hear our prayer.

Leader	Open *their hearts* to your grace and truth.
People	Lord, hear our prayer.

Leader	Keep *them* in the faith and communion of your holy Church.
People	Lord, hear our prayer.

Leader	Teach *them* to love others in the power of the Spirit.
People	Lord, hear our prayer.

Leader	Send *them* into the world in witness to your love.
People	Lord, hear our prayer.

Leader	Bring *them* to the fullness of your peace and glory.
People	Lord, hear our prayer.

The Celebrant says

Grant, O Lord, that all who are baptized into the death of Jesus Christ your Son may live in the power of his resurrection and look for him to come again in glory; who lives and reigns now and for ever. *Amen.*

Thanksgiving over the Water

The Celebrant blesses the water, first saying

	The Lord be with you.
People	And also with you.
Celebrant	Let us give thanks to the Lord our God.
People	It is right to give him thanks and praise.

Celebrant

We thank you, Almighty God, for the gift of water. Over it the Holy Spirit moved in the beginning of creation. Through it you led the children of Israel out of their bondage in Egypt into the land of promise. In it your Son Jesus received the baptism of John and was anointed by the Holy Spirit as the Messiah, the Christ, to lead us, through his death and resurrection, from the bondage of sin into everlasting life.

We thank you, Father, for the water of Baptism. In it we are buried with Christ in his death. By it we share in his resurrection. Through it we are reborn by the Holy Spirit. Therefore in joyful obedience to your Son, we bring into his fellowship those who come to him in faith, baptizing them in the Name of the Father, and of the Son, and of the Holy Spirit.

At the following words, the Celebrant touches the water

Now sanctify this water, we pray you, by the power of your Holy Spirit, that those who here are cleansed from sin and born again may continue for ever in the risen life of Jesus Christ our Savior.

To him, to you, and to the Holy Spirit, be all honor and glory, now and for ever. *Amen.*

Consecration of the Chrism

The Bishop may then consecrate oil of Chrism, placing a hand on the vessel of oil, and saying

Eternal Father, whose blessed Son was anointed by the Holy Spirit to be the Savior and servant of all, we pray you to consecrate this oil, that those who are sealed with it may share in the royal priesthood of Jesus Christ; who lives and reigns with you and the Holy Spirit, for ever and ever. *Amen.*

The Baptism

Each candidate is presented by name to the Celebrant, or to an assisting priest or deacon, who then immerses, or pours water upon, the candidate, saying

_____, I baptize you in the Name of the Father, and of the Son, and of the Holy Spirit. *Amen.*

When this action has been completed for all candidates, the Bishop or Priest, at a place in full sight of the congregation, prays over them, saying

Let us pray.

Heavenly Father, we thank you that by water and the Holy Spirit you have bestowed upon *these* your *servants* the forgiveness of sin, and have raised *them* to the new life of grace. Sustain *them*, O Lord, in your Holy Spirit. Give *them* an inquiring and discerning heart, the courage to will and to persevere, a spirit to know and to love you, and the gift of joy and wonder in all your works. *Amen.*

Then the Bishop or Priest places a hand on the person's head, marking on the forehead the sign of the cross [using Chrism if desired] and saying to each one

_____, you are sealed by the Holy Spirit in Baptism and marked as Christ's own for ever. *Amen.*

Or this action may be done immediately after the administration of the water and before the preceding prayer.

When all have been baptized, the Celebrant says

Let us welcome the newly baptized.

Celebrant and People

We receive you into the household of God. Confess the faith of Christ crucified, proclaim his resurrection, and share with us in his eternal priesthood.

If Confirmation, Reception, or the Reaffirmation of Baptismal Vows is not to follow, the Peace is now exchanged

Celebrant	The peace of the Lord be always with you.
People	And also with you.

At Confirmation, Reception, or Reaffirmation

The Bishop says to the congregation

Let us now pray for *these persons* who *have* renewed *their* commitment to Christ.

Silence may be kept.

Then the Bishop says

Almighty God, we thank you that by the death and resurrection of your Son Jesus Christ you have overcome sin and brought us to yourself, and that by the sealing of your Holy Spirit you have bound us to your service. Renew in *these* your *servants* the covenant you made with *them* at *their* Baptism. Send *them* forth in the power of that Spirit to perform the service you set before *them;* through Jesus Christ your Son our Lord, who lives and reigns with you and the Holy Spirit, one God, now and for ever. *Amen.*

For Confirmation

The Bishop lays hands upon each one and says

Strengthen, O Lord, your servant _____ with your Holy Spirit; empower *him* for your service; and sustain *him* all the days of *his* life. *Amen.*

or this

Defend, O Lord, your servant _____ with your heavenly grace, that *he* may continue yours for ever, and daily increase in your Holy Spirit more and more, until *he* comes to your everlasting kingdom. *Amen.*

For Reception

_____ , we recognize you as a member of the one holy catholic and apostolic Church, and we receive you into the fellowship of this Communion. God, the Father, Son, and Holy Spirit, bless, preserve, and keep you. *Amen.*

For Reaffirmation

_____ , may the Holy Spirit, who has begun a good work in you, direct and uphold you in the service of Christ and his kingdom. *Amen.*

Then the Bishop says

Almighty and everliving God, let your fatherly hand ever be over *these* your *servants;* let your Holy Spirit ever be with *them;* and so lead *them* in the knowledge and obedience of your Word, that *they* may serve you in this life, and dwell with you in the life to come, through Jesus Christ our Lord. *Amen.*

The Peace is then exchanged

Bishop	The peace of the Lord be always with you.
People	And also with you.

At the Eucharist

The service then continues with the Prayers of the People or the Offertory of the Eucharist, at which the Bishop, when present, should be the principal Celebrant.

If there is no celebration of the Eucharist, the service concludes with the Lord's Prayer, a prayer by the celebrant, and a blessing.

Emergency Baptism

In case of emergency, any baptized person may administer Baptism according to the following form.

Using the given name of the one to be baptized (if known), pour water on him or her, saying

I baptize you in the Name of the Father, and of the Son, and of the Holy Spirit.

The Lord's Prayer is then said.

Other prayers, such as the following, may be added

Heavenly Father, we thank you that by water and the Holy Spirit you have bestowed upon this your servant the forgiveness of sin and have raised *him* to the new life of grace. Strengthen *him*, O Lord, with your presence, enfold *him* in the arms of your mercy, and keep *him* safe for ever.

If the newly baptized person is at the point of death, say this Commendation over him or her:

Depart, O Christian soul, out of this world;
In the Name of God the Father Almighty who created you;
In the Name of Jesus Christ who redeemed you;
In the Name of the Holy Spirit who sanctifies you.
May your rest be this day in peace,
    and your dwelling place in the Paradise of God.

Other prayers for the dying are on pages 157–165.

Report the facts to the chaplain when you can.

Bautismo en Caso de Emergencia

En caso de emergencia, cualquier persona bautizada puede administrar el Bautismo, de acuerdo con la siguiente fórmula.

Usando el nombre propio de la persona que va a ser bautizada (si se conoce), se derrama agua sobre la cabeza, diciendo:

Yo te bautizo en el Nombre del Padre, y del Hijo y del Espíritu Santo.

Después se dice el Padre Nuestro.

Pueden añadirse otras oraciones, como la siguiente:

Padre celestial, te damos gracias porque por medio del agua y del Espíritu Santo has concedido a este tu siervo el pardón de los pecados y le has levantado a la nueva vida de gracia. Fortalécele, oh Señor, con tu presencia, estréchale en los brazos du tu misericordia y protégele para siempre.

Si la persona que ha sido bautizada está agonizando, diga sobre ella la oración comendatoria:

Parte, oh alma cristiana, de este mundo;
En el nombre de Dios Padre todopoderoso, que te creó;
En el nombre de Jesucristo, que te redimió;
En el nombre del Espíritu Santo, que te santifica.
Que en este día, tu descanso sea en paz,
   Y tu morada en el Paraíso de Dios.

Otras oraciones por los moribundos se encuentran en las páginas 157–165.

Informe al capellán de este hecho lo antes posible.

ABOUT THE HOLY EUCHARIST

The Holy Eucharist is the Church's principal act of worship on the Lord's Day (Sunday), on other great feast days, and on special occasions. The service consists of two major parts, the Ministry (or Liturgy) of the Word, in which we hear God's word read and preached; and the Celebration of the Holy Communion, in which we proclaim Christ's death and resurrection, and are united to him and to one another in the Sacrament of his Body and Blood.

In the Episcopal Church, the celebrant (presiding minister) at the Eucharist is always a bishop or priest. All baptized persons present, however, share in the celebration. In keeping with the teaching of the Scripture, the elements used are bread and wine.

The Episcopal Church teaches that Christ is truly present at the Eucharist in accordance with his promise (Matthew 28:20). He is present in the midst of his people when they gather in his name, in the persons of the ministers who lead the service, in the reading and preaching of his word, and, in a special way, in the consecrated bread and wine (Matthew 18:20; Luke 24:30–35; John 6:53–56; 1 Corinthians 10:16–17). The Church does not try to explain Christ's presence in this sacrament, but it believes that it is a "real presence."

PREPARING FOR HOLY COMMUNION

It is the teaching of the Church, and of the New Testament, that those who come to the Eucharist should examine their lives, repent of their sins, and be in love and charity with all people. If you do not confess your sins and thank God for his blessings every day in your prayers, it is especially important to do so before coming to Communion. In addition to praying in your own words, you may find it helpful to read some of the Psalms, Readings, and Prayers suggested on pages 87, 65, and 37 of this book. For further information about repentance, see page 150.

THE HOLY EUCHARIST: RITE TWO

The Word of God

A hymn, psalm, or anthem may be sung.

The people standing, the Celebrant says

Blessed be God: Father, Son, and Holy Spirit.

People   And blessed be his kingdom, now and for ever. Amen.

In place of the above, from Easter Day through the Day of Pentecost

Celebrant   Alleluia. Christ is risen.
People   The Lord is risen indeed. Alleluia.

In Lent and on other penitential occasions

Celebrant   Bless the Lord who forgives all our sins.
People   His mercy endures for ever.

The Celebrant may say

Almighty God, to you all hearts are open, all desires known, and from you no secrets are hid: Cleanse the thoughts of our hearts by the inspiration of your Holy Spirit, that we may perfectly love you, and worthily magnify your holy Name; through Christ our Lord. *Amen.*

In place of the preceding prayer, the Confession of Sin on page 134 may be said.

When appointed, the following hymn or some other song of praise is sung or said, all standing

Glory to God in the highest,
  and peace to his people on earth.

Lord God, heavenly King,
almighty God and Father,
  we worship you, we give you thanks,
  we praise you for your glory.

Lord Jesus Christ, only Son of the Father,
Lord God, Lamb of God,
you take away the sin of the world:
    have mercy on us;
you are seated at the right hand of the Father:
    receive our prayer.

For you alone are the Holy One,
you alone are the Lord,
you alone are the Most High,
    Jesus Christ,
    with the Holy Spirit,
    in the glory of God the Father. Amen.

On other occasions the following is used

Lord, have mercy.		Kyrie eleison.
Christ, have mercy.	*or*	Christe eleison.
Lord, have mercy.		Kyrie eleison.

or this

Holy God,
Holy and Mighty,
Holy Immortal One, *Have mercy upon us.*

The Prayer of the Day

The Celebrant says to the people

	The Lord be with you.
People	And also with you.
Celebrant	Let us pray.

The Celebrant says the Prayer.
People   Amen.

The Lessons

The people sit. One or two Lessons, as appointed, are read, the Reader first saying

A Reading (Lesson) from _____ .

A citation giving chapter and verse may be added.

After each Reading, the Reader may say

The Word of the Lord.
People   Thanks be to God.

Or the reader may say Here ends the Reading (Epistle).

Silence may follow.

A Psalm, hymn, or anthem may follow each Reading.

Then, all standing, the Deacon or a Priest reads the Gospel, first saying

The Holy Gospel of our Lord Jesus Christ
according to _____ .
People   Glory to you, Lord Christ.

After the Gospel, the Reader says

The Gospel of the Lord.
People   Praise to you, Lord Christ.

The Sermon

On Sundays and other Major Feasts there follows, all standing

The Nicene Creed

We believe in one God,
    the Father, the Almighty,
    maker of heaven and earth,
    of all that is, seen and unseen.

We believe in one Lord, Jesus Christ,
    the only Son of God,
    eternally begotten of the Father,
    God from God, Light from Light,
    true God from true God,
    begotten, not made,
    of one Being with the Father.
    Through him all things were made.

For us and for our salvation
  he came down from heaven:
by the power of the Holy Spirit
  he became incarnate from the Virgin Mary,
  and was made man.
For our sake he was crucified under Pontius Pilate;
  he suffered death and was buried.
  On the third day he rose again
    in accordance with the Scriptures;
  he ascended into heaven
    and is seated at the right hand of the Father.
He will come again in glory to judge the living and the dead,
  and his kingdom will have no end.

We believe in the Holy Spirit, the Lord, the giver of life,
  who proceeds from the Father and the Son.
  With the Father and the Son he is worshiped and glorified.
  He has spoken through the Prophets.
  We believe in one holy catholic and apostolic Church.
  We acknowledge one baptism for the forgiveness of sins.
  We look for the resurrection of the dead,
    and the life of the world to come. Amen.

The Prayers of the People

Prayer is offered with intercession for

The Universal Church, its members, and its mission
The Nation and all in authority
The welfare of the world
The concerns of the local community
Those who suffer and those in any trouble
The departed (with commemoration of a saint when appropriate)
Either of the following or some other form may be used.

Form A

The Leader and People pray responsively

In peace, we pray to you, Lord God.

Silence

For all people in their daily life and work;
For our families, friends, and neighbors, and for those who are alone.

For this community, the nation, and the world;
For all who work for justice, freedom, and peace.

For the just and proper use of your creation;
For the victims of hunger, fear, injustice, and oppression.

For all who are in danger, sorrow, or any kind of trouble;
For those who minister to the sick, the friendless, and the needy.

For the peace and unity of the Church of God;
For all who proclaim the Gospel, and all who seek the Truth.

For [_____, our Presiding Bishop, and _____ (_____) our Bishop(s); and for] all bishops and other ministers;
For all who serve God in his Church.

For the special needs and concerns of this congregation.

Silence

The People may add their own petitions

Hear us, Lord;
For your mercy is great.

We thank you, Lord, for all the blessings of this life.

Silence

The People may add their own thanksgivings

We will exalt you, O God our King;
And praise your Name for ever and ever.

We pray for all who have died, that they may have a place in your eternal kingdom.

Silence

People may add their own petitions

Lord, let your loving-kindness be upon them;
Who put their trust in you.

The Celebrant concludes with this or some other prayer

Lord Jesus Christ, you said to your apostles, "Peace I give to you; my own peace I leave with you." Regard not our sins, but the faith of your Church, and give to us the peace and unity of that heavenly City, where with the Father and the Holy Spirit you live and reign, now and for ever. *Amen.*

Form B

Leader

Let us pray for the holy Church of God in every place, and for all people in their needs.

For your Church throughout the world, that it may serve you in faith and unity, in the fellowship of the Holy Spirit, we pray to you, O Lord.
Lord, have mercy.

For all bishops, chaplains, and other ministers of Christ, we pray to you, O Lord.
Lord, have mercy.

That all nations may receive the Gospel of Christ, and serve you in peace, we pray to you, O Lord.
Lord, have mercy.

For the leaders of our country, especially _____ our President [and for the leaders of our allies (especially _____ and _____)], we pray to you, O Lord.
Lord, have mercy.

That all people may be delivered from oppression, hunger, fear, and injustice, we pray to you, O Lord.
Lord, have mercy.

For ourselves, our families, friends, and companions, we pray to you, O Lord.
Lord, have mercy.

For the sick, the wounded, the suffering, the bereaved, and all in special need (particularly _____), we pray to you, O Lord.
Lord, have mercy.

For all who have died (especially _____), we pray to you, O Lord.
Lord, have mercy.

Silence

The Celebrant concludes with this or some other Prayer

Grant, O Lord, that we may serve you faithfully in this life, and finally enter with [_____ and] all your saints into the joy of your heavenly kingdom; through your Son Jesus Christ our Lord. *Amen.*

If there is no celebration of the Communion, or if a priest is not available, the service concludes with the singing of a hymn (if desired), the Lord's Prayer, and with either the Grace or a blessing, or with the exchange of the Peace.

But if Communion is to be administered from the reserved Sacrament, the service continues on page 143.

Confession of Sin

A Confession of Sin is said here if it has not been said earlier. On occasion, the Confession may be omitted.

The Deacon or Celebrant says

Let us confess our sins against God and our neighbor.

Silence may be kept.

Minister and People

Most merciful God,
we confess that we have sinned against you
in thought, word, and deed,
by what we have done,
and by what we have left undone.

We have not loved you with our whole heart;
we have not loved our neighbors as ourselves.
We are truly sorry and we humbly repent.
For the sake of your Son Jesus Christ,
have mercy on us and forgive us;
that we may delight in your will,
and walk in your ways,
to the glory of your Name. Amen.

The Bishop when present, or the Priest, stands and says

Almighty God have mercy on you, forgive you all your sins through
our Lord Jesus Christ, strengthen you in all goodness, and by the
power of the Holy Spirit keep you in eternal life. *Amen.*

*A deacon or lay person using the preceding form substitutes "us" for "you"
and "our" for "your."*

The Peace

All stand. The Celebrant says to the people

	The peace of the Lord be always with you.
People	And also with you.

Then the Ministers and People may greet one another in the name of the Lord.

The Holy Communion

The Celebrant may begin the Offertory with a sentence of Scripture.

During the Offertory, a hymn, psalm, or anthem may be sung.

*Representatives of the congregation bring the people's offerings of bread and
wine, and money or other gifts, to the deacon or celebrant. The people stand
while the offerings are presented and placed on the Altar.*

The Great Thanksgiving

Eucharistic Prayer A
*The people remain standing. The Celebrant, whether bishop or priest, faces
them and sings or says*

	The Lord be with you.
People	And also with you.

Celebrant	Lift up your hearts.
People	We lift them to the Lord.

Celebrant	Let us give thanks to the Lord our God.
People	It is right to give him thanks and praise.

Then, facing the Holy Table, the Celebrant proceeds

It is right, and a good and joyful thing, always and everywhere to give thanks to you, Father Almighty, Creator of heaven and earth.

Here a Proper Preface is sung or said on all Sundays, and on other occasions as appointed.

Therefore we praise you, joining our voices with Angels and Archangels and with all the company of heaven, who for ever sing this hymn to proclaim the glory of your Name:

Celebrant and people

Holy, holy, holy Lord, God of power and might,
heaven and earth are full of your glory.
    Hosanna in the highest.
Blessed is he who comes in the name of the Lord.
    Hosanna in the highest.

The people stand or kneel.
Then the Celebrant continues

Holy and gracious Father: In your infinite love you made us for yourself; and, when we had fallen into sin and become subject to evil and death, you, in your mercy, sent Jesus Christ, your only and eternal Son, to share our human nature, to live and die as one of us, to reconcile us to you, the God and Father of all.

He stretched out his arms upon the cross, and offered himself in obedience to your will, a perfect sacrifice for the whole world.

At the following words concerning the bread, the Celebrant is to hold it or lay a hand upon it; and at the words concerning the cup, to hold or place a hand upon the cup and any other vessel containing wine to be consecrated.

On the night he was handed over to suffering and death, our Lord Jesus Christ took bread; and when he had given thanks to you, he broke it, and gave it to his disciples, and said, "Take, eat: This is my Body, which is given for you. Do this for the remembrance of me."

After supper he took the cup of wine; and when he had given thanks, he gave it to them, and said, "Drink this, all of you: This is my Blood of the new Covenant, which is shed for you and for many for the forgiveness of sins. Whenever you drink it, do this for the remembrance of me."

Therefore we proclaim the mystery of faith:

Celebrant and People
Christ has died.
Christ is risen.
Christ will come again.

The Celebrant continues
We celebrate the memorial of our redemption, O Father, in this sacrifice of praise and thanksgiving. Recalling his death, resurrection, and ascension, we offer you these gifts.

Sanctify them by your Holy Spirit to be for your people the Body and Blood of your Son, the holy food and drink of new and unending life in him. Sanctify us also that we may faithfully receive this holy Sacrament, and serve you in unity, constancy, and peace; and at the last day bring us with all your saints into the joy of your eternal kingdom.

All this we ask through your Son Jesus Christ. By him, and with him, and in him, in the unity of the Holy Spirit all honor and glory is yours, Almighty Father, now and for ever. *AMEN.*

And now as our Savior
Christ has taught us,
we are bold to say,

As our Savior Christ
has taught us,
we now pray,

People and Celebrant

Our Father, who art in heaven,
   hallowed be thy Name,
     thy kingdom come,
     thy will be done,
       on earth as it is in heaven.
Give us this day our daily bread.
And forgive us our trespasses,
   as we forgive those
     who trespass against us.
And lead us not into temptation,
   But deliver us from evil.
For thine is the kingdom,
   and the power, and the glory,
   for ever and ever. Amen.

Our Father in heaven,
   hallowed be your Name,
     your kingdom come,
     your will be done
       on earth as in heaven.
Give us today our daily bread.
Forgive us our sins
   as we forgive those
     who sin against us.
Save us from the time of trial,
   and deliver us from evil.
For the kingdom, the power,
   and the glory are yours,
   now and for ever. Amen.

The Breaking of the Bread

The Celebrant breaks the consecrated Bread.
A period of silence is kept.

Then may be sung or said

[Alleluia.] Christ our Passover is sacrificed for us;
Therefore let us keep the feast. [*Alleluia.*]

In Lent, Alleluia is omitted, and may be omitted at other times except during
Easter Season.

In place of, or in addition to, the preceding, some other suitable anthem may
be used.

Facing the people, the Celebrant says the following Invitation

The gifts of God for the People of God.
and may add Take them in remembrance that Christ died for you,
and feed on him in your hearts by faith, with thanksgiving.

The ministers receive the Sacrament in both kinds, and then immediately deliver it to the people.

The Bread and the Cup are given to the communicants with these words

The Body (Blood) of our Lord Jesus Christ keep you in everlasting life. [*Amen.*]

or with these words

The Body of Christ, the bread of heaven. [*Amen.*]
The Blood of Christ, the cup of salvation. [*Amen.*]

During the ministration of Communion, hymns, psalms, or anthems may be sung.

When necessary, the Celebrant consecrates additional bread and wine, using the form on page 141.

After Communion, the Celebrant says

Let us pray.

Celebrant and People

Eternal God, heavenly Father,
you have graciously accepted us as living members
of your Son our Savior Jesus Christ,
and you have fed us with spiritual food
in the Sacrament of his Body and Blood.
Send us now into the world in peace,
and grant us strength and courage
to love and serve you
with gladness and singleness of heart;
through Christ our Lord. Amen.

or the following

Almighty and everliving God,
we thank you for feeding us with the spiritual food
of the most precious Body and Blood
of your Son our Savior Jesus Christ;

and for assuring us in these holy mysteries
that we are living members of the Body of your Son,
and heirs of your eternal kingdom.
And now, Father, send us out
to do the work you have given us to do,
to love and serve you
as faithful witnesses of Christ our Lord.
To him, to you, and to the Holy Spirit,
be honor and glory, now and for ever. Amen.

The Bishop when present, or the Priest, may bless the people.

The Deacon, or the Celebrant, dismisses them with these words

	Let us go forth in the name of Christ.
People	Thanks be to God.
or this	
Deacon	Go in peace to love and serve the Lord.
People	Thanks be to God.
or this	
Deacon	Let us go forth into the world, rejoicing in the power of the Spirit.
People	Thanks be to God.
or this	
Deacon	Let us bless the Lord.
People	Thanks be to God.

From the Easter Vigil through the Day of Pentecost "Alleluia, alleluia" may be added to any of the dismissals.

The People respond
Thanks be to God. Alleluia, alleluia.

ADDITIONAL DIRECTIONS

The Prayers, Psalms, and Lessons used at celebrations of the Holy Eucharist are ordinarily those appointed in the Book of Common Prayer. When the situation warrants, however, other Propers may be used, or a selection may be made from material included in this book.

When it is necessary to shorten the service, the form provided on page 142 is used.

The persons specifically appointed by the chaplain should normally be assigned the reading of the lessons which precede the Gospel, and may lead the Prayers of the People.

Lay persons specifically licensed by the Bishop for the Armed Services may administer the chalice when invited to do so by the celebrant.

In the absence of a priest, a licensed lay reader may lead the first part of the service, concluding it as described on page 134.

Appropriate parts of the service may be sung as desired. The texts of anthems are to be from Holy Scripture, or from the Book of Common Prayer, or from texts congruent with them. Hymns may be from *The Hymnal 1982,* from the *Book of Worship for United Forces,* or from this book.

FORM FOR CONSECRATING
ADDITIONAL ELEMENTS

Hear us, O heavenly Father, and with your Word and Holy Spirit bless and sanctify this bread (wine) that it, also, may be the Sacrament of the precious Body (Blood) of your Son Jesus Christ our Lord, who took bread (the cup) and said, "This is my Body (Blood)." *Amen.*

THE HOLY EUCHARIST:
A SHORTER FORM

This form is intended to enable military chaplains of the Episcopal Church to celebrate the Eucharist under conditions which make it not feasible to use the full form given in the Book of Common Prayer and on pages 128–140 of this book.

1. A passage from the Gospel, appropriate to the day or occasion, is read.

2. After the Reading, the chaplain may comment on it briefly.

3. Suitable prayers may be offered. One of the forms of the Prayers of the People on pages 131–134 may be used.

4. The Confession of Sin, page 134, may be said.

5. The service continues with the Peace and Offertory, page 135.

In place of the usual postcommunion prayer, the chaplain may use the following:

Gracious Father, we give you praise and thanks for this Holy Communion of the Body and Blood of your beloved Son Jesus Christ, the pledge of our redemption; and we pray that it may bring us forgiveness of our sins, strength in our weakness, and everlasting salvation; through Jesus Christ our Lord. *Amen.*

In cases of necessity, the chaplain may begin with the Offertory, but it is desirable that a brief passage from the Gospel (such as Reading no. 20, page 74) be read first.

COMMUNION FROM
THE RESERVED SACRAMENT

This form is intended for use by military chaplains of the Episcopal Church in administering the already consecrated Sacrament to individuals who, for reasonable cause, cannot be present at a public celebration of the Eucharist.

It is intended for use by duly authorized and licensed lay eucharistic ministers in administering Communion to congregations and individuals where there is no chaplain.

When used with individuals, the service begins with a passage of Scripture appropriate to the day or occasion. A brief comment on the Reading may follow, and suitable prayers may be offered.

When used with a congregation, the service begins with the Liturgy of the Word of God, page 128, as far as the end of the Prayers of the People.

The service then continues as follows:

Confession of Sin

A Confession of Sin may be said.

The Minister says

Let us confess our sins against God and our neighbor.

Silence may be kept.

Minister and People

Most merciful God,
we confess that we have sinned against you
in thought, word, and deed,
by what we have done,
and by what we have left undone.
We have not loved you with our whole heart;
we have not loved our neighbors as ourselves.
We are truly sorry and we humbly repent.

For the sake of your Son Jesus Christ,
have mercy on us and forgive us;
that we may delight in your will,
and walk in your ways,
to the glory of your Name. Amen.

The Chaplain then says

Almighty God have mercy upon you, forgive you all your sins
through our Lord Jesus Christ, strengthen you in goodness, and
by the power of the Holy Spirit keep you in eternal life. *Amen.*

*A lay eucharistic minister using the preceding form substitutes "us" for "you"
and "our" for "your."*

The Peace

The Peace is then exchanged

Minister	The peace of the Lord be always with you.
People	And also with you.

The Communion

The Lord's Prayer is said, the Minister first saying

Let us pray in the words our Savior Christ has taught us.

People and Celebrant

Our Father, who art in heaven,
   hallowed be thy Name,
   thy kingdom come,
   thy will be done,
     on earth as it is in heaven.
Give us this day our daily bread.
And forgive us our trespasses,
   as we forgive those
    who trespass against us.
And lead us not into temptation,
   But deliver us from evil.
For thine is the kingdom,
   and the power, and the glory,
   for ever and ever. Amen.

Our Father in heaven,
   hallowed be your Name,
   your kingdom come,
   your will be done
     on earth as in heaven.
Give us today our daily bread.
Forgive us our sins
   as we forgive those
    who sin against us.
Save us from the time of trial,
   and deliver us from evil.
For the kingdom, the power,
   and the glory are yours,
   now and for ever. Amen.

The Minister may say the following Invitation

The Gifts of God for the People of God.
and may add Take them in remembrance that Christ died for you, and feed on him in your hearts by faith, with thanksgiving.

The Sacrament is administered with the following words

The Body (Blood) of our Lord Jesus Christ keep you in everlasting life. [*Amen.*]

or with these words

The Body of Christ, the bread of heaven. [*Amen.*]
The Blood of Christ, the cup of salvation. [*Amen.*]

or, in Spanish

El Cuerpo (la Sangre) de nuestro Señor Jesucristo te guarde en la vida eterna. [*Amén.*]

o con estas

El Cuerpo de Cristo, pan del cielo. [*Amén.*]
La Sangre de Cristo, cáliz de salvación. [*Amén.*]

After Communion, the Lay Eucharistic Minister and People say one of the postcommunion prayers on pages 139–140, after which the Minister dismisses the people.

When this form is used with individuals, however, the following postcommunion prayer may be used instead

Gracious Father, we give you praise and thanks for this Holy Communion of the Body and Blood of your beloved Son Jesus Christ, the pledge of our redemption; and we pray that it may bring us forgiveness of our sins, strength in our weakness, and everlasting salvation; through Jesus Christ our Lord. *Amen.*

The service then concludes with a blessing by the chaplain or with this dismissal

Let us bless the Lord.
Thanks be to God.

WHEN HOLY COMMUNION
IS NOT AVAILABLE

Wherever they may be, members of the Church should always try to receive Holy Communion regularly. It is the most sacred means which Christ has given us to unite us to himself and to his Church. If you are stationed where there is no Episcopal chaplain, it may be possible for you to attend a nearby civilian parish church. In many overseas areas, you may receive the sacraments from clergy of other Anglican Churches. These Churches have the same faith as the Episcopal Church, their services are very similar to ours, and you may look to them as to your own Church. The Episcopal Church is also in communion with several other Churches in Europe and Asia. You will also be welcomed in the Evangelical Lutheran Church in America (ELCA) and some other Lutheran Churches, both overseas and in North America.

It may well happen, however, that you are stationed in a place where none of these opportunities is open to you. You may, and indeed should, attend some Christian service of worship each week. Yet you will miss receiving Holy Communion in the way that is familiar to you. Men and women in the service wonder whether they may receive Communion in some other Church. Many chaplains of various Christian bodies will be willing to administer to you. Whether or not you wish to receive their ministrations will depend on several factors.

It is not generally recommended that you receive any sacramental rites in another Church (a) unless the priest or minister of that Church is willing for you to do so, (b) unless you are actually cut off from the ministrations of your own Church for a long period, (c) unless the faith of the other denomination is based on Holy Scripture and the Creeds, and its practice of the sacraments is comparable to your own, and (d) unless you can participate in its worship in an honest and prayerful manner without compromising your own faith and Church loyalty.

If you are attending the Lord's Supper or Mass in another Church, and are not going to communicate, it is recommended that while others are receiving Communion, you remain in silent prayer. The prayer "For Communion with Christ," given below may be useful to you at such times.

WHEN YOU CANNOT ATTEND WORSHIP

On Sundays, if you cannot attend a service of worship, it is suggested that you perform the following devotions privately.

1. Read the Lessons and Psalm for the Day appointed in the Book of Common Prayer, or one or more of the Bible Readings and Psalms given in this book. See pages 65 and 87 for suggestions.

2. Say the Apostles' Creed (unless you have already said it in your morning prayers).

3. Say one of the forms of the Prayers of the People (pages 131–134) and, if desired, the Confession of Sin (page 134).

4. Then say this prayer:

A Prayer for Communion with Christ

In union, O Lord, with your faithful people at every altar of your Church, where the Holy Eucharist is now being celebrated, I desire to offer to you praise and thanksgiving. I remember your death, Lord Christ; I proclaim your resurrection; I await your coming in glory. And since I cannot receive you today in the Sacrament of your Body and Blood, I beseech you to come spiritually into my heart. Cleanse and strengthen me with your grace, Lord Jesus, and let me never be separated from you. May I live in you, and you in me, in this life and in the life to come. Amen.

The General Thanksgiving (page 59) may also be used.

5. Conclude your devotions with these words:

To Christ our Lord who loves us, and washed us in his own blood, and made us a kingdom of priests to serve his God and Father, to him be glory and dominion for ever and ever. Amen.

THE TEN COMMANDMENTS

1. I am the Lord your God who brought you out of bondage. You shall have no other gods but me.

2. You shall not make for yourself any idol.

3. You shall not invoke with malice the Name of the Lord your God.

4. Remember the Sabbath Day and keep it holy.

5. Honor your father and your mother.

6. You shall not commit murder.

7. You shall not commit adultery.

8. You shall not steal.

9. You shall not be a false witness.

10. You shall not covet anything that belongs to your neighbor.

Exodus 20; Deuteronomy 5

THE SUMMARY OF THE LAW

Jesus said, "The first commandment is this: Hear, O Israel: The Lord our God is the only Lord. Love the Lord your God with all your heart, with all your soul, with all your mind, and with all your strength. The second is this: Love your neighbor as yourself. There is no other commandment greater than these." *Mark 12:29–31*

DECÁLOGO

1. Yo soy el Señor tu Dios que te sacó de la servidumbre.

2. No te harás imagen alguna.

3. No invocarás en falso el Nombre del Señor tu Dios.

4. Recuerda el día del sábado para santificarlo.

5. Honra a tu padre y a tu madre.

6. No asesinarás.

7. No cometerás adulterio.

8. No robarás.

9. No darás testimonio falso.

10. No codiciarás nada de lo que pertenezca a tu prójimo.

Exodo 20; Deuteronomio 5

SUMARIO DE LA LEY

Jesús dijo: "El primer mandamiento es éste: Escucha, Israel: El Señor nuestro Dios es el único Señor. Amaras al Señor tu Dios con todo tu corazón, con toda tu alma, con toda tu mente y con todas tus fuerzas. El segundo es éste: Amarás a tu prójimo como a ti mismo. No hay otro mandamiento mayor que éstos." *San Marcos 12:29–31*

ABOUT PENANCE AND RECONCILIATION

REPENTANCE AND FORGIVENESS

All us fall into sin at one time or another. Our sins may appear very small, or very large, but in either case they grieve God, they directly or indirectly harm others, and they reduce our own integrity and spiritual strength. To ignore or disregard the fact of sin is unrealistic, because sin causes great harm both to individuals and to society. On the other hand, to think about our sins continually can lead to depression, and sometimes to further wrongdoing.

God through Christ has given us the remedy for sin. This remedy is penitence or repentance. By regular penitence a Christian can increasingly overcome his or her sins, shortcomings, and weaknesses; one can become more pleasing to God and to one's neighbors. Penitence has several stages. First, there is self-examination, the process of looking back and seeing which of our thoughts, words, and actions have been sinful. Second, there is confession, in which we admit our sins and honestly accept the guilt of having done wrong. In confession we go on to ask God to forgive us. Third, there is reparation, or willingness to restore and make good our relation to others, and to forgive those who have sinned against us. God promises forgiveness to those who truly repent.

The New Testament (1 Corinthians 11:28) teaches us that before coming to communion we should examine our lives and conduct, and the Book of Common Prayer re-echoes this warning (pages 316–317). Our private self-examination and prayer for forgiveness prepares us to participate in the general Confession of Sin frequently used at the Eucharist and to receive Absolution (the priest's declaration of forgiveness). We need not wait until Sunday morning to examine our consciences, however. The faithful Christian will find it best to make a brief self-examination every evening, and to pray for God's forgiveness of the sins and shortcomings of the past day.

CONFESSION TO A PRIEST

Unfortunately, we sometimes fall into more serious sin, and our consciences continue to bother us. It is for this reason that the Book of Common Prayer provides that we may confess our sins privately, in the presence of a priest. By doing this, we receive the benefit of the priest's counsel and spiritual guidance, as well as individual assurance of God's pardon and absolution.

Those who desire to make their confession in this way, but have never done so before, should consult with the priest beforehand for guidance. Such a confession is a most solemn act, and is performed in a place of privacy. The priest is strictly bound to treat all that is said in complete confidence.

CONFESSION TO A LAY PERSON

When necessary, such as when someone is badly wounded or dying, or is in serious depression, and there is no priest available, a lay person may hear the confession of another Christian. A lay person who does this is bound by the same rule of complete confidence, and must never, under any circumstances, reveal anything that has been said in the confession. The form given below is used, but in place of the Absolution (which a lay person may not pronounce), the Declaration of Forgiveness given at the end of the form is used.

THE RECONCILIATION OF A PENITENT

The Penitent begins

Bless me, for I have sinned.

The Priest says

The Lord be in your heart and upon your lips that you may truly and humbly confess your sins: In the Name of the Father, and of the Son, and of the Holy Spirit. *Amen.*

Penitent

I confess to Almighty God, to his Church, and to you, that I have sinned by my own fault in thought, word, and deed, in things done and left undone; especially _____ . For these and all other sins which I cannot now remember, I am truly sorry. I pray God to have mercy on me. I firmly intend amendment of life, and I humbly beg forgiveness of God and his Church, and ask you for counsel, direction, and absolution.

Here the Priest may offer counsel, direction, and comfort.

The Priest then pronounces this absolution

Our Lord Jesus Christ, who has left power to his Church to absolve all sinners who truly repent and believe in him, of his great mercy forgive you all your offenses; and by his authority committed to me, I absolve you from all your sins: In the Name of the Father, and of the Son, and of the Holy Spirit. *Amen.*

or this

Our Lord Jesus Christ, who offered himself to be sacrificed for us to the Father, and who conferred power on his Church to forgive sins, absolve you through my ministry by the grace of the Holy Spirit, and restore you in the perfect peace of the Church. *Amen.*

The Priest adds

The Lord has put away all your sins.

Penitent   Thanks be to God.

The Priest concludes

Go (or abide) in peace, and pray for me, a sinner.

DECLARATION OF FORGIVENESS
TO BE USED BY A DEACON OR LAY PERSON

Our Lord Jesus Christ, who offered himself to be sacrificed for us to the Father, forgives your sins by the grace of the Holy Spirit. *Amen.*

MINISTRATION TO THE SICK
OR WOUNDED

It is natural to turn to God in prayer when suffering from sickness or wounds. Such times can be opportunities for spiritual growth. God can help us learn to endure the pain, annoyance, loneliness, and boredom which come to us. A number of the Psalms, Bible Readings, and prayers in this book are appropriate for use at such times. See pages 87 and 65 for Psalms and Readings, and page 37 for prayers. These may be used by the person alone, or by a chaplain or lay reader visiting the sick.

If you are sick or wounded, and your conscience is bothering you, you should speak to the chaplain. If you wish to confess your sins privately, the form on pages 152–153 will be used. Otherwise, the chaplain will lead you in saying the general Confession of Sin on page 134 and give you absolution.

Then, if you desire it, the chaplain will perform the Church's special ministry of healing by laying hands on you (and anointing you with oil), using the following form:

Laying on of Hands and Anointing

If oil for the Anointing of the Sick is to be blessed, the Priest says

O Lord, holy Father, giver of health and salvation: Send your Holy Spirit to sanctify this oil; that, as your holy apostles anointed many that were sick and healed them, so may those who in faith and repentance receive this holy unction be made whole; through Jesus Christ our Lord, who lives and reigns with you and the Holy Spirit, one God, for ever and ever. *Amen.*

The following anthem is said

Savior of the world, by your cross and precious blood you have redeemed us;

Save us, and help us, we humbly beseech you, O Lord.

The Priest then lays hands upon the sick person, and says one of the following

_____ , I lay my hands upon you in the Name of the Father, and of the Son, and of the Holy Spirit, beseeching our Lord Jesus Christ to sustain you with his presence, to drive away all sickness of body and spirit, and to give you that victory of life and peace which will enable you to serve him both now and evermore. *Amen.*

or this

_____ , I lay my hands upon you in the Name of our Lord and Savior Jesus Christ, beseeching him to uphold you and fill you with his grace, that you may know the healing power of his love. *Amen.*

If the person is to be anointed, the Priest dips a thumb in the holy oil, and makes the sign of the cross on the sick person's forehead (or elsewhere if necessary), saying

_____ , I anoint you with oil in the Name of the Father, and of the Son, and of the Holy Spirit. *Amen.*

The Priest may add

As you are outwardly anointed with this holy oil, so may our Father grant you the inward anointing of the Holy Spirit. Of his great mercy, may he forgive you your sins, release you from suffering, and restore you to wholeness and strength. May he deliver you from all evil, preserve you in all goodness, and bring you to everlasting life; through Jesus Christ our Lord. *Amen.*

In cases of necessity, a deacon or lay person may perform the anointing, using oil blessed by a bishop or priest.

If Communion is not to follow, the Lord's Prayer is now said.

The Priest concludes

The Almighty Lord, who is a strong tower to all who put their trust in him, to whom all things in heaven, on earth, and under the earth bow and obey: Be now and evermore your defense, and make you know and feel that the only Name under heaven given for health and salvation is the Name of our Lord Jesus Christ. *Amen.*

Holy Communion

In administering Holy Communion to the sick or wounded, the chaplain may either (1) celebrate the Eucharist, using the form on page 142, or (2) give Communion from the reserved Sacrament, using the form on page 143. In either case, if the laying on of hands (and anointing) has immediately preceded, the chaplain begins the Communion rite with the Peace.

FOR THE DYING

When Facing Death Yourself

If you are about to die, say the Lord's Prayer and the Apostles' Creed. In your own words, ask God to forgive the sins you have committed, to have mercy on all persons you have wronged or injured, and to forgive all who have sinned against you. Pray for your family and any others who especially deserve your prayers. Sum up your prayers with words such as these:

Almighty God, I entrust all who are dear to me to your never-failing care and love, for this life and the life to come; knowing that you are doing for them better things than I can desire or pray for; through Jesus Christ our Lord. Amen.

As your earthly life comes to a close, use these words which Christ used:

Father, into your hands I commend my spirit.

Cuando en Peligro de Muerte

Si usted está a punto de morir, diga el Padre Nuestro y el Credo de los Apóstoles. Usando sus propias palabras, pida perdón a Dios por todos sus pecados, que tenga misericordia sobre todos aquéllos que usted ha engañado o herido y que perdone a todos aquéllos que han pecado contra usted. Ore par su familia y por todos aquéllos que especialmente merecen sus oraciones. Resuma sus oraciones con frases como la siguiente:

Omnipotente Dios, encomiendo a aquéllos que me son queridos a tu fiel cuidado y amor, en esta vida y la venidera; sabiendo que estás haciendo por ellos mejores cosas que las que pueda desear o suplicar; por Jesucristo nuestro Señor. Amén.

Al llegar tu vida al final, usa esta palabras que Cristo dijo:

Padre, en tus manos encomiendo mi espíritu.

Commendation of the Dying

If you are with someone who is dying, say the Lord's Prayer. If possible, have the person say it with you. If the person cannot speak, say the prayer for him or her. (People who are dying can often hear even if they seem unconscious.) You may also say the Creed (inside the front cover).

If the person is not baptized, and desires to be, use the form for Emergency Baptism on pages 124–126.

If there is time, you may read a suitable Psalm, such as Psalm 23 (pages 89–90 or 105), or a Bible Reading, such as "Who will separate us?" (page 82).

The Litany at the Time of Death, pages 164–165, may also be said.

At the moment of death, this commendation is said over a dying Christian:

Depart, O Christian soul, out of this world;
In the Name of God the Father Almighty who created you;
In the Name of Jesus Christ who redeemed you;
In the Name of the Holy Spirit who sanctifies you.
May your rest be this day in peace,
and your dwelling place in the Paradise of God.

When the person has died, say this commendatory prayer:

Into your hands, O merciful Savior, we commend your servant _____ . Acknowledge, we humbly beseech you, a sheep of your own fold, a lamb of your own flock, a sinner of your own redeeming. Receive him into the arms of your mercy, into the blessed rest of everlasting peace, and into the glorious company of the saints in light. *Amen.*

May *his* soul and the souls of all the departed, through the mercy of God, rest in peace. *Amen.*

The following commendation may be used for one who does not profess the Christian faith:

Almighty God, creator of us all, and lover of the human race: We commend our brother (sister) _____ into your merciful hands. Deliver *him* from all fear, strengthen *him* with your presence, and give *him* peace; through Jesus Christ our Lord. *Amen.*

ACT OF CONTRITION AND
COMMENDATION OF THE DYING
(ROMAN CATHOLIC)

If the person who is dying is a Roman Catholic, remind him or her to make an Act of Perfect Contrition, using one of the following or similar words. If necessary, say the words yourself and have the person say them after you.

O my God, I am sorry for my sins because I have offended you. I know I should love you above all things. Forgive me my sins. Help me to do penance, to do better, and to avoid anything that might lead me to sin. Amen.

or this,

Jesus, I love you and am sorry for having offended you. Amen.

If the person cannot speak, or appears to be unconscious or dead, speak directly into the person's ear. Tell him or her that you will recite an Act of Contrition, and to try to make this prayer with you, either in words or in their heart. Then say the shorter form given above. The following prayer may also be used:

Hail Mary, full of grace, the Lord is with thee. Blessed art thou among women, blessed is the fruit of thy womb, Jesus. Holy Mary, mother of God, pray for us sinners, now and at the hour of our death. Amen.

If there is time, you may read a suitable Psalm, such as Psalm 23 (pages 89–90 or 105), or a Bible Reading, such as "Who will separate us?" (page 82).

At the moment of death, say this commendation:

In the name of God the Father Almighty who created you,
in the name of Jesus Christ, Son of the living God,
    who suffered for you,

in the name of the Holy Spirit, who was poured out
    upon you,
go forth, faithful Christian.
May you live in peace this day,
may your home be with God in Zion,
with Mary the virgin Mother of God,
with Joseph, and all the angels and saints.

CONFESSION FOR THE CRITICALLY ILL (JEWISH)

Lord My God and God of my ancestors, I acknowledge that in Your hand alone is my recovery or my death. May it be Your will that I be completely healed. Yet if it be Your will that I die, then I shall accept death lovingly at Your hands. May my death be atonement for all my sins, transgressions, and wrongs that I have done before You. May I receive a portion of that goodness that is stored up for the righteous. Make me to know the path of life, the fullness of blissful joy in Your Presence at Your right hand forever more.

O You who are the Father of the fatherless and the guardian of the widow, protect my beloved family, whose souls are linked to mine. Into Your hand I commend my spirit; You have redeemed me, O God of truth. Amen and Amen.

When the end is approaching:

The Lord is King; the Lord was King; the Lord shall reign forever and ever. (*Said three times.*)

Blessed is His glorious kingdom forever and ever. (*Said three times.*)

The Lord, He is God. (*Said seven times.*)

Hear, O Israel: the Lord is our God; the Lord is One!

She-ma Yis-ra-eil: A-do-nai E-lo-hei-nu; A-do-nai e-chad!

ISLAMIC EMERGENCY MINISTRATION

If a dying person desires religious ministration when no chaplain is available, anyone may repeat with him/her the following prayers:

A. *The Shahada:* There is no God but Allah and Mohammed is the messenger of Allah. Amen.

B. *Prayers for the Dying*

1. Allah is great! *(repeat four times)*

2. O God, I ask of Thee a perfect faith, a sincere assurance, a reverent heart, a remembering tongue, a good conduct of commendation, and a true repentance, repentance before death, rest at death, and forgiveness and mercy after death, clemency at the reckoning, victory in paradise and escape from the fire, by Thy mercy, O mighty One; O Forgiver, Lord increase me in knowledge and join me unto good.

3. O Lord, may the end of my life be the best of it; may my closing acts be my best acts, and may the best of my days be the day when I shall meet Thee. Amen.

C. *In the event of death the individual's eyes should be gently closed, and the following prayer repeated:*

Allah! Make his/her affair light, render easy what he/she is going to face after this, bless him/her with Thy vision, and make his/her new abode better for him/her than the one he/she has left behind. Amen.

LITANY AT THE TIME OF DEATH

This Litany may be said by one or more persons when someone is dying, or shortly afterwards. It may also be used at funeral or memorial services.

God the Father,
Have mercy on your servant.

God the Son,
Have mercy on your servant.

God the Holy Spirit,
Have mercy on your servant.

Holy Trinity, one God,
Have mercy on your servant.

From all evil, from all sin, from all tribulation,
Good Lord, deliver him.

By your holy Incarnation, by your Cross and Passion, by your precious Death and Burial,
Good Lord, deliver him.

By your glorious Resurrection and Ascension, and by the Coming of the Holy Spirit,
Good Lord, deliver him.

We sinners beseech you to hear us, Lord Christ: That it may please you to deliver the soul of your servant from the power of evil, and from eternal death,
We beseech you to hear us, good Lord.

That it may please you mercifully to pardon all *his* sins.
We beseech you to hear us, good Lord.

That it may please you to grant *him* a place of refreshment and everlasting blessedness,
We beseech you to hear us, good Lord.

That it may please you to give *him* joy and gladness in your kingdom, with your saints in light,
We beseech you to hear us, good Lord.

Jesus, Lamb of God:
Have mercy on him.

Jesus, bearer of our sins:
Have mercy on him.

Jesus, redeemer of the world:
Give him *your peace.*

Lord have mercy.
Christ have mercy.
Lord have mercy.

Officiant and People

Our Father, who art in heaven,
   hallowed be thy Name,
   thy kingdom come,
   thy will be done,
     on earth as it is in heaven.
Give us this day our daily bread.
And forgive us our trespasses,
   as we forgive those
     who trespass against us.
And lead us not into temptation,
   But deliver us from evil.

Our Father in heaven,
   hallowed be your Name,
   your kingdom come,
   your will be done
     on earth as in heaven.
Give us today our daily bread.
Forgive us our sins
   as we forgive those
     who sin against us.
Save us from the time of trial,
   and deliver us from evil.

The Leader then says this prayer

Let us pray.

Deliver your servant, _____, O' Sovereign Lord Christ, from all evil, and set *him* free from every bond; that *he* may rest with all your saints in the eternal habitations; where with the Father and the Holy Spirit you live and reign, one God, for ever and ever. *Amen.*

If the person is at the point of death, continue with the Commendation on page 158.

If the person has already died, continue with the Commendatory Prayer "Into your hands" on page 158.

BURIAL OF THE DEAD
AND MEMORIAL SERVICES

Funeral Services and Memorial Services are ordinarily conducted by a chaplain. When the person who has died was a communicant of the Church, it is appropriate that the Episcopal chaplain celebrate the Eucharist at such services.

In the absence of a chaplain, a lay reader or other member of the Church may lead the service, using the form for "A Service of Worship" on page 112. Prayer no. 71 ("O God of grace and glory"), page 57, is appropriate for an opening prayer. For suggested Readings and Psalms, see pages 65 and 87. For the Prayers of the People, the Litany at the Time of Death may be used, or the leader may choose other prayers.

A licensed lay reader may also use the form on page 491 of the Book of Common Prayer.

Emergency Burial on Land or at Sea

Put some earth on the body, or cast the body reverently into the sea, and say these or similar words

In sure and certain hope of the resurrection to eternal life through our Lord Jesus Christ, we commend to Almighty God our brother (sister) _____, and we commit *his* body to the ground (or to the deep); earth to earth, ashes to ashes, dust to dust. The Lord bless *him* and keep *him,* the Lord make his face to shine upon *him* and be gracious to *him,* the Lord lift up his countenance upon *him* and give *him* peace. *Amen.*

Then say these prayers
Our Father...

Rest eternal grant to *him,* O Lord;
And let light perpetual shine upon him.

May *his* soul, and the souls of all the departed, through the mercy of God, rest in peace. *Amen.*

Hymns

1

Edward Perronet (1726–1792), alt.

1 All hail the power of Jesus' Name!
  Let angels prostrate fall;
  bring forth the royal diadem,
  and crown him Lord of all!

2 Sinners, whose love can ne'er forget
  the wormwood and the gall,
  go, spread your trophies at his feet,
  and crown him Lord of all!

3 Let every kindred, every tribe,
  on this terrestrial ball,
  to him all majesty ascribe,
  and crown him Lord of all!

2

John Newton (1725–1807), alt.; st. 5, from
A Collection of Sacred Ballads, 1790;
compiled by Richard Broaddus and Andrew Broaddus

1 Amazing grace! how sweet the sound,
    that saved a wretch like me!
  I once was lost but now am found,
    was blind but now I see.

2 'Twas grace that taught my heart to fear,
    and grace my fears relieved;
  how precious did that grace appear
    the hour I first believed!

3 The Lord has promised good to me,
    his word my hope secures;
  he will my shield and portion be
    as long as life endures.

4 Through many dangers, toils, and snares,
    I have already come;
  'tis grace that brought me safe thus far,
    and grace will lead me home.

5 When we've been there ten thousand years,
    bright shining as the sun,
we've no less days to sing God's praise
    than when we'd first begun.

3   Jan Struther (1901–1953)

1 Lord of all hopefulness, Lord of all joy,
    whose trust, ever childlike, no cares could destroy,
    be there at our waking, and give us, we pray,
    your bliss in our hearts, Lord, at the break of the day.

2 Lord of all eagerness, Lord of all faith,
    whose strong hands were skilled at the plane and the lathe,
    be there at our labors, and give us, we pray,
    your strength in our hearts, Lord, at the noon of the day.

3 Lord of all gentleness, Lord of all calm,
    whose voice is contentment, whose presence is balm,
    be there at our sleeping, and give us, we pray,
    your peace in our hearts, Lord, at the end of the day.

4   Fanny J. Crosby (1820–1915)

1 Blessed assurance, Jesus is mine!
    O what a foretaste of glory divine!
    Heir of salvation, purchase of God,
    Born of His spirit, washed in His blood.

    *Refrain: This is my story, this is my song,
            Praising my savior all the day long;
            This is my story, this is my song,
            Praising my savior all the day long.*

2 Perfect submission, perfect delight,
    Visions of rapture now burst on my sight;
    Angels descending, bring from above
    Echoes of mercy, whispers of love.

            Refrain

³ Perfect submission, all is at rest,
   I in my savior am happy and blest;
   Watching and waiting, looking above,
   Filled with His goodness, lost in His love.

     Refrain

5

Frederick William Faber (1814–1863), alt.

¹ Faith of our fathers! living still
      in spite of dungeon, fire and sword:
O how our hearts beat high with joy,
      whene'er we hear that glorious word:

Refrain: *Faith of our fathers, holy faith!*
              We will be true to thee till death.

² Faith of our fathers! faith and prayer
      shall win all nations unto thee;
and through the truth that comes from God,
      mankind shall then indeed be free.

     Refrain

³ Faith of our fathers! we will love
      both friend and foe in all our strife:
and preach thee, too, as love knows how,
      by kindly deeds and virtuous life.

     Refrain

6

Civilla D. Martin (1860–1948)

¹ Why should I feel discouraged,
   Why should the shadows come,
   Why should my heart be lonely,
   And long for heav'n and home;
   When Jesus is my portion?
   My constant friend is He:

Refrain: *His eye is on the sparrow,*
    And I know He watches me;
    His eye is on the sparrow,
    and I know He watches me.
    I sing because I'm happy,
    I sing because I'm free;
    For His eye is on the sparrow,
    And I know He watches me.

2 "Let not your heart be troubled,"
   His tender word I hear,
   And resting on His goodness,
   I lose my doubts and fears;
   Though by the path He leadeth,
   But one step I may see;

        Refrain

3 When ever I am tempted,
   When ever clouds arise,
   When songs give place to sighing,
   When hope within me dies,
   I draw the closer to Him,
   From care He sets me free;

        Refrain

7   Reginald Heber (1783–1826), alt.

1 Holy, holy, holy! Lord God Almighty!
    Early in the morning our song shall rise to thee:
   Holy, holy, holy! Merciful and mighty,
    God in three Persons, blessèd Trinity.

2 Holy, holy, holy! All the saints adore thee,
    casting down their golden crowns around the glassy sea;
   cherubim and seraphim falling down before thee,
    which wert, and art, and evermore shalt be.

3 Holy, holy, holy! Lord God Almighty!
   All thy works shall praise thy Name, in earth, and sky, and sea;
Holy, holy, holy! Merciful and mighty,
   God in three Persons, blessèd Trinity.

8

Horatio Spafford (1828–1888)

1 When peace, like a river, attendeth my way,
   When sorrows like seabillows roll;
Whatever my lot, thou hast taught me to say,
   It is well, it is well with my soul.

*Refrain: It is well with my soul,
             It is well, it is well with my soul.*

2 Though Satan should buffet, though trials should come,
   Let this blest assurance control,
That Christ has regarded my helpless estate,
   And has shed His own blood for my soul.

               Refrain

3 And, Lord, haste the day when the faith shall be sight,
   The clouds be rolled back as a scroll,
The trump shall resound and the Lord shall descend,
   "Even so," it is well with my soul.

               Refrain

9

John Oxenham (1852–1941), alt.

1 In Christ there is no East or West,
   in him no South or North,
but one great fellowship of love
   throughout the whole wide earth.

2 Join hands, disciples of the faith,
   whate'er your race may be!
Who serves my Father as his child
   is surely kin to me.

³ In Christ now meet both East and West,
    in him meet South and North,
all Christly souls are one in him,
    throughout the whole wide earth.

10

Cesareo Gabarain

Estribillo: Juntos como hermanos, miembros de una Iglesia,
           vamos caminando al encuentro del Señor.

¹ Un largo caminar por el desierto bajo el sol;
   no podemos avanzar sin la ayuda del Señor.

        Estribillo

² Unidos al rezar, unidos en una canción,
   viviremos nuestra fe con la ayuda del Señor.

        Estribillo

³ La Iglesia en marcha está a un mundo nuevo vamos ya
   donde reinará el amor, donde reinará la paz.

        Estribillo

11

African-American spiritual

¹ Let us break bread together on our knees;

      when I fall on my knees,
      with my face to the rising sun,
      O Lord, have mercy on me.

² Let us drink wine together on our knees;

      when I fall on my knees,
      with my face to the rising sun,
      O Lord, have mercy on me.

3 Let us praise God together on our knees;

when I fall on my knees,
with my face to the rising sun,
O Lord, have mercy on me.

12   Liturgy of St. James; para. Gerard Moultrie (1829–1885)

1 Let all mortal flesh keep silence,
   and with fear and trembling stand;
   ponder nothing earthly-minded,
   for with blessing in his hand
   Christ our God to earth descendeth,
   our full homage to demand.

2 King of kings, yet born of Mary,
   as of old on earth he stood,
   Lord of lords in human vesture,
   in the Body and the Blood
   he will give to all the faithful
   his own self for heavenly food.

3 At his feet the six-winged seraph;
   cherubim with sleepless eye
   veil their faces to the Presence,
   as with ceaseless voice they cry,
   "Alleluia, alleluia!
   Alleluia, Lord Most High!"

13   Isaac Watts (1674–1748), alt.; para. of Psalm 90

1 O God, our help in ages past,
      our hope for years to come,
   our shelter from the stormy blast,
      and our eternal home:

2 Under the shadow of thy throne
     thy saints have dwelt secure;
sufficient is thine arm alone,
     and our defense is sure.

3 O God, our help in ages past,
     our hope for years to come,
be thou our guide while life shall last,
     and our eternal home.

14   Joachim Neander (1650–1680); tr. *Hymnal 1940*, alt.

1 Praise to the Lord, the Almighty, the King of creation;
   O my soul, praise him, for he is thy health and salvation:
      join the great throng,
      psaltery, organ, and song,
   sounding in glad adoration.

2 Praise to the Lord, who doth prosper thy way and defend thee;
   surely his goodness and mercy shall ever attend thee;
      ponder anew
      what the Almighty can do,
   who with his love doth befriend thee.

3 Praise to the Lord! O let all that is in me adore him!
   All that hath life and breath come now with praises before him!
      Let the amen
      sound from his people again;
   gladly for ever adore him.

15   American folk hymn, ca. 1835

1 What wondrous love is this,
     O my soul, O my soul!
What wondrous love is this,
     O my soul!

What wondrous love is this
that caused the Lord of bliss
   to lay aside his crown
     for my soul, for my soul,
   to lay aside his crown
     for my soul.

2 To God and to the Lamb,
  I will sing, I will sing,
to God and to the Lamb,
  I will sing.
To God and to the Lamb
who is the great I AM,
   while millions join the theme,
     I will sing, I will sing,
   while millions join the theme
     I will sing.

3 And when from death I'm free,
  I'll sing on, I'll sing on,
and when from death I'm free,
  I'll sing on.
And when from death I'm free
I'll sing and joyful be,
   and through eternity
     I'll sing on, I'll sing on,
   and through eternity
     I'll sing on, I'll sing on.

16

Isaac Watts (1674–1748)

1 When I survey the wondrous cross
   where the young Prince of Glory died,
   my richest gain I count but loss,
and pour contempt on all my pride.

2 Forbid it, Lord, that I should boast,
    save in the cross of Christ, my God:
all the vain things that charm me most,
    I sacrifice them to his blood.

3 See, from his head, his hands, his feet
    sorrow and love flow mingled down!
Did e'er such love and sorrow meet,
    or thorns compose so rich a crown?

4 Were the whole realm of nature mine,
    that were an offering far too small;
love so amazing, so divine,
    demands my soul, my life, my all.

17   Traditional

1 I want Jesus to walk with me (walk with me);
  I want Jesus to walk with me (walk with me);
  all along my pilgrim journey, Lord,
  I want Jesus to walk with me (walk with me).

2 In my trials, Lord, walk with me (walk with me);
  in my trials, Lord, walk with me (walk with me);
  when the shades of life are falling, Lord,
  I want Jesus to walk with me (walk with me).

3 In my sorrows, Lord, walk with me (walk with me);
  in my sorrows, Lord, walk with me (walk with me);
  when my heart within is aching, Lord,
  I want Jesus to walk with me (walk with me).

18   Cesareo Gabarain

1 Tú has venido a la orilla,
  no has buscado ni a sabios ni a ricos,
  tan sólo quieres que yo te siga.

Estribillo: *Señor, me has mirado a los ojos*
y sonriendo has dicho mi nombre;
en la arena he dejado mi barca;
junto a ti buscaré otro mar.

2 Tú sabes bien lo que tengo:
En mi barca no hay oro ni espadas,
tan sólo redes y mi trabajo.

Estribillo

3 Tú necesitas mis manos,
mi cansancio que a otros descanse,
amor que quiera seguir amando.

Estribillo

4 Tú, pescador de otros mares,
ansia eterna de almas que esperan,
amigo bueno, que así me llamas.

Estribillo

19

Eleanor Farjeon (1881–1965), alt.

1 Morning has broken
like the first morning,
blackbird has spoken
like the first bird.
Praise for the singing!
Praise for the morning!
Praise for them, springing
fresh from the Word!

2 Sweet the rain's new fall
sunlit from heaven,
like the first dewfall
on the first grass.

Praise for the sweetness
of the wet garden,
sprung in completeness
where his feet pass.

3 Mine is the sunlight!
Mine is the morning
born of the one light
Eden saw play!
Praise with elation,
praise every morning,
God's re-creation
of the new day!

20

William Chatterton Dix (1837–1898)

1 Alleluia! sing to Jesus!
his the scepter, his the throne;
Alleluia! his the triumph,
his the victory alone;
Hark! the songs of peaceful Zion
thunder like a mighty flood;
Jesus out of every nation
hath redeemed us by his blood.

2 Alleluia! King eternal,
thee the Lord of lords we own:
Alleluia! born of Mary,
earth thy footstool, heaven thy throne:
thou within the veil hast entered,
robed in flesh, our great High Priest:
thou on earth both Priest and Victim
in the eucharistic feast.

3 Alleluia! sing to Jesus!
his the scepter, his the throne;
Alleluia! his the triumph,
his the victory alone;

Hark! the songs of holy Zion
thunder like a mighty flood;
Jesus out of every nation
hath redeemed us by his blood.

21   John Francis Wade (1711–1786); tr. Frederick Oakeley (1802–1880) and others

1 O come, all ye faithful,
    joyful and triumphant,
O come ye, O come ye to Bethlehem;
    come, and behold him,
    born the King of angels;

Refrain: O come, let us adore him,
            Christ the Lord.

2 God from God,
    Light from Light eternal,
lo! he abhors not the Virgin's womb;
    only-begotten
    Son of God the Father;

            Refrain

3 Yea, Lord, we greet thee,
    born this happy morning;
Jesus, to thee be glory given;
    Word of the Father,
    now in flesh appearing;

            Refrain

22   Luke 2:8–20; adapt. John W. Work, Jr. (1871–1925)

Refrain: Go, tell it on the mountain
            over the hills and everywhere;
            go, tell it on the mountain,
            that Jesus Christ is born.

¹ While shepherds kept their watching
    o'er silent flocks by night,
Behold throughout the heavens
    there shown a holy light.

Refrain

² The shepherds feared and trembled,
    when lo! above the earth,
Rang out the angel chorus
    that hailed the Savior's birth.

Refrain

³ Down in a lowly manger
    the humble Christ was born,
And God sent us salvation
    that blessed Christmas morn.

Refrain

23   Joseph Mohr (1792–1848); tr. John Freeman Young (1820–1885)

¹ Silent night, holy night,
all is calm, all is bright
round yon virgin mother and child.
Holy infant, so tender and mild,
sleep in heavenly peace.

² Silent night, holy night,
shepherds quake at the sight,
glories stream from heaven afar,
heavenly hosts sing alleluia;
Christ, the Savior, is born!

³ Silent night, holy night,
Son of God, love's pure light
radiant beams from thy holy face,
with the dawn of redeeming grace,
Jesus, Lord, at thy birth.

24   Latin, 14th cent.; tr. *Lyra Davidica*, 1708, alt. St. 4, Charles Wesley (1707–1788)

1 Jesus Christ is risen today,
   our triumphant holy day,
   who did once upon the cross,
   suffer to redeem our loss. Alleluia!

2 Hymns of praise then let us sing,
   unto Christ, our heavenly King,
   who endured the cross and grave,
   sinners to redeem and save. Alleluia!

3 But the pains which he endured,
   our salvation have procured;
   now above the sky he's King,
   where the angels ever sing. Alleluia!

4 Sing we to our God above
   praise eternal as his love;
   praise him, all ye heavenly host,
   Father, Son, and Holy Ghost. Alleluia!

25   Latin, 1632; tr. Robert Campbell (1814–1868), alt.

1 At the Lamb's high feast we sing
   praise to our victorious King,
   who hath washed us in the tide
   flowing from his piercèd side;
   praise we him, whose love divine
   gives his sacred Blood for wine,
   gives his Body for the feast,
   Christ the victim, Christ the priest.

2 Mighty victim from on high,
   hell's fierce powers beneath thee lie;
   thou hast conquered in the fight,
   thou hast brought us life and light:
   now no more can death appall,
   now no more the grave enthrall;

thou hast opened paradise,
and in thee thy saints shall rise.

3 Easter triumph, Easter joy,
these alone do sin destroy.
From sin's power do thou set free
souls new-born, O Lord, in thee.
Hymns of glory, songs of praise,
Father, unto thee we raise:
risen Lord, all praise to thee
with the Spirit ever be.

26

1 Eternal Father, strong to save,
Whose arm hath bound the restless wave,
Who bidd'st the mighty ocean deep
Its own appointed limits keep;
Oh, hear us when we cry to thee,
For those in peril on the sea!

2 Lord, guard and guide all those who fly
And those who on the ocean ply;
Be with our troops upon the land,
And all who for their country stand:
Be with these guardians day and night
And may their trust be in thy might.

3 Eternal Father, grant, we pray,
To all Marines, both night and day,
The courage, honor, strength, and skill
Their land to serve, thy law fulfill
Be thou the shield forevermore
From every peril to the Corps.

4 Eternal Father, Lord of hosts,
Watch o'er all those who guard our coasts.
Protect them from the raging seas
And give them light and life and peace.

Grant them from thy great throne above
The shield and shelter of thy love.

5 God, Who dost still the restless foam,
Protect the ones we love at home.
Provide that they should always be
By thine own grace both safe and free.
O Father, hear us when we pray
For those we love so far away.

6 Creator, Father, who first breathed
In us the life that we received,
By power of thy breath restore
The ill, and those with wounds of war.
Bless those who give their healing care,
That life and laughter all may share.

27

Katherine Lee Bates (1859–1929), alt.

1 O beautiful for spacious skies,
    for amber waves of grain,
for purple mountain majesties
    above the fruited plain!
America! America!
    God shed his grace on thee,
and crown thy good with brotherhood
    from sea to shining sea.

2 O beautiful for heroes proved
    in liberating strife,
who more than self their country loved,
    and mercy more than life!
America! America!
    God mend thine every flaw,
confirm thy soul in self-control,
    thy liberty in law.

3 O beautiful for patriot dream
    that sees beyond the years

thine alabaster cities gleam,
  undimmed by human tears!
America! America!
  God shed his grace on thee,
and crown thy good with brotherhood
  from sea to shining sea.

28

Francis Scott Key (1779–1843)

1 O say can you see, by the dawn's early light,
  what so proudly we hailed at the twilight's last gleaming,
  whose broad stripes and bright stars, through the perilous fight,
  o'er the ramparts we watched, were so gallantly streaming?
  And the rockets' red glare, the bombs bursting in air,
  gave proof through the night that our flag was still there.
  O say does that star-spangled banner yet wave
  o'er the land of the free and the home of the brave?

2 O thus be it ever, when freemen shall stand
  between their loved homes and the war's desolation!
  Blest with victory and peace, may the heaven-rescued land
  praise the Power that hath made and preserved us a nation!
  Then conquer we must, when our cause it is just,
  and this be our motto, "In God is our trust."
  And the star-spangled banner in triumph shall wave
  o'er the land of the free and the home of the brave!

29

Samuel Francis Smith (1808–1895)

1 My country, 'tis of thee,
  sweet land of liberty,
    of thee I sing;
  land where my fathers died,
  land of the pilgrims' pride,
  from every mountainside
    let freedom ring.

2 Let music swell the breeze,
 and ring from all the trees
  sweet freedom's song;
 let mortal tongues awake,
 let all that breathe partake,
 let rocks their silence break,
  the sound prolong.

3 Our fathers' God, to thee,
 author of liberty,
  to thee we sing;
 long may our land be bright
 with freedom's holy light;
 protect us by thy might,
  great God, our King.

The Church Year

The Church Year begins with the **Season of Advent**, which starts on the Sunday that falls on or closest to November 30. Advent is a Latin word meaning "coming," and during this season we look forward to Jesus' coming in glory at the end of time and to the coming celebration of his birth. Christmas comes in the week following the Fourth Sunday of Advent.

Christmas Season lasts twelve days, from Christmas Day (December 25) until the Epiphany (January 6). Christmas Season includes one or two Sundays.

Epiphany Season extends from January 6 (a celebration of the coming of the Wise Men to the infant Jesus) until Ash Wednesday, and includes from four to nine Sundays. The First Sunday after the Epiphany is the feast of the Baptism of Christ. Epiphany is a Greek word meaning "showing," and in this season we remember many of the ways in which Jesus showed himself to be the Messiah, the Son of God.

The **Season of Lent** lasts from Ash Wednesday until Easter Day. It includes six Sundays and forty weekdays. Lent is the time in which we examine our lives and prepare to renew our baptismal vows at Easter. (See the Baptismal Covenant on page 118.)

Holy Week is the last week of Lent. It begins on the Sunday of the Passion (Palm Sunday) and includes Maundy Thursday, Good Friday, and Holy Saturday.

Easter Season lasts fifty days, from Easter Day — the holiest day in the Church Year — through the Day of Pentecost (which means "fiftieth"). This season includes seven "Sundays of Easter" and the feast of the Ascension on the fortieth day (always a Thursday). The Day of Pentecost is a celebration of the gift of the Holy Spirit to the Church. During Easter Season we rejoice, not only because Jesus rose from the dead, but because in Baptism he has made us sharers in his resurrection and given us his Holy Spirit.

The **Season after Pentecost** (also called Ordinary Time) continues until the next Advent, and includes more than twenty Sundays. The First Sunday after Pentecost is also called Trinity Sunday.

About the Episcopal Church

The Episcopal Church is one of forty-four national and regional churches of the Anglican Communion. Most of these churches, in 166 countries worldwide, trace their beginnings to the work of missionaries sent by the Church of England. All together, there are more than 80 million Anglicans.

Each of these national or regional churches is independent, but they often work closely together in mission and ministry, and they look for spiritual leadership to the Archbishop of Canterbury. The Church of England itself traces its history back to missionaries who arrived in the British Isles from Gaul (France), Egypt, and Italy in the third through the sixth centuries.

The Episcopal Church in the United States became independent of the Church of England in 1786, shortly after the American Revolution. Perhaps not surprisingly, its method of governance is similar to that of the Federal Government. The church's General Convention, which meets every three years, consists of two houses: the House of Bishops and the House of Deputies (which consists of elected members of the clergy and laity). All changes in church law and policy must be agreed to by both houses.

The faith of the Episcopal Church is the traditional Christian faith handed down from the time of the New Testament. While some churches require their members to accept beliefs that are not mentioned in the Bible, or to interpret the Bible in a particular way, the Anglican churches believe that the Bible itself contains all teaching necessary to salvation.

The Episcopal Church confesses this biblical faith in its worship, proclaiming Jesus Christ to be true God and true Man, who — by his birth, ministry, death, resurrection, and ascension — brought salvation to the world. We also acknowledge that God is Trinity: Father, Son, and Holy Spirit. These basic beliefs are summarized in the two creeds used in our worship, the Apostles' Creed (inside the front cover) and the Nicene Creed (page 130).

The Episcopal Church also accepts the traditional view that the sacraments are saving events. We believe, for example, that in Holy Baptism we are truly born again in Christ, and that in the Eucharist (Holy Communion) Christ is truly present under the forms of bread and wine. We also believe that Christ is present in the teaching of his word, and whenever two or three are gathered together in his name (Matthew 18:20).

The chief ministers of the church are the bishops, whose task is to unify the church and to guard the faith which has been handed down to it. Each bishop has been ordained and consecrated by other bishops, in a line that traces back to the time of the apostles. This continuity of the faith, guarded by the bishops, is called "apostolic succession," and it signifies the continuity of the church today with the church of the New Testament. The two other orders of ordained ministers are the priests (also called presbyters) and deacons.

By virtue of their baptism, lay people have a place of major importance and responsibility in the Episcopal Church — in its ministry, in its government, and in its worship. At church services lay people regularly assist in various ways. Some lay ministries require a license from the bishop; others do not.

The Bishop Suffragan for Federal Service regularly licenses many men and women as "lay readers." These persons assist the chaplain in appropriate ways, and, in the chaplain's absence, lead services of worship. Such licensing is done with the approval of the Senior Chaplain, and after extensive study and training.